the Self-Love Experiment

and a passion for helping others identify and pursue what they truly want."

—Lori Deschene, founder of TinyBuddha.com and author of
Tiny Buddha: Simple Wisdom for Life's Hard Questions

"Shannon shares her story of vulnerability and victory and emerges as a radiant example of what is possible with a mental makeover. Shannon gives you an easy-to-follow road map to lasting happiness, joy, and inner transformation. People say happiness is an inside job—this is the ultimate how-to manual."

—Amy Leigh Mercree, author of
The Spiritual Girl's Guide to Dating

"Shannon's blazing one hell of a self-love trail for others to show up, release fear, and live life, fully. You know, one where your dreams come true, and we live happily ever after in love, with ourselves! The world needs this self-love injection. And so do you."

—Emma Mildon, bestselling author of
The Soul Searcher's Handbook and *The Evolution of Goddess*

"Shannon is an absolute Goddess. She's a beautiful example of what is possible when you free yourself from self-criticism, blame, and guilt, and choose love instead. I am in total adoration of this woman, and that's because of how in love she is with herself, the world, and life! Thank you, Shannon, for being such a light. Readers, you are in for a treat!"

—Melissa Wells, eating psychology coach and bestselling author
of *The Goddess Revolution: Make Peace with Food,
Love Your Body and Reclaim Your Life*

"*The Self-Love Experiment* is the book I wish I'd had in my twenties. And my thirties. Now more than ever, we as women need to rise up and empower ourselves and each other. Shannon's book is like the necessary guidebook we need to get ourselves there. Self-love can seem elusive, but Shannon has broken it down in easy-to-digest lessons."

—Andrea Owen, author of *52 Ways to Live a Kick-Ass Life:*
BS-Free Wisdom to Ignite Your Inner Badass and
Live the Life You Deserve

"One of the freshest voices in mental health and wellness, Shannon is on a mission to empower others to be true to themselves and live their full potential."

—Marci Shimoff, *New York Times* bestselling author of *Happy*
for No Reason and coeditor of *Chicken Soup for the Woman's Soul*

"Shannon Kaiser inspires people to ditch what doesn't serve them and follow their paths to true joy and satisfaction."

—mindbodygreen

"Shannon Kaiser is an incredible woman on a mission to help people find peace, happiness, and fulfillment in their lives. Her desire to serve others shines through all of her work."

—Gabrielle Bernstein, *New York Times* bestselling author of
May Cause Miracles

SHANNON KAISER

the

Self-Love

Experiment

Fifteen Principles for
Becoming More Kind,
Compassionate, and
Accepting of Yourself

A TARCHERPERIGEE BOOK

An imprint of Penguin Random House LLC
375 Hudson Street
New York, New York 10014

TarcherPerigee with tp colophon is a registered trademark of
Penguin Random House LLC.

Most TarcherPerigee books are available at special quantity discounts for bulk purchase for sales promotions, premiums, fund-raising, and educational needs. Special books or book excerpts also can be created to fit specific needs. For details, write: SpecialMarkets@penguinrandomhouse.com.

Library of Congress Cataloging-in-Publication Data

Names: Kaiser, Shannon, author.
Title: The self-love experiment : fifteen principles for becoming more kind, compassionate, and accepting of yourself / Shannon Kaiser.
Description: New York : TarcherPerigee, 2017. | Includes bibliographical references.
Identifiers: LCCN 2017014368 (print) | LCCN 2017024608 (ebook) | ISBN 9780143130697 (paperback) | ISBN 9781524704520 (ebook)
Subjects: LCSH: Self-esteem. | Self-actualization (Psychology) | Happiness. | BISAC: SELF-HELP / Personal Growth / Happiness. | SELF-HELP / Personal Growth / Self-Esteem. | SELF-HELP / Personal Growth / General.
Classification: LCC BF697.5.S46 K35 2017 (ebook) | LCC BF697.5.S46 (print) | DDC 158.1—dc23
LC record available at https://lccn.loc.gov/2017014368

Printed in the United States of America
3 5 7 9 10 8 6 4 2

Book design by Pauline Neuwirth, Neuwirth & Associates, Inc.

This book is dedicated to
YOU, DEAR READER,
For showing up for yourself, for listening to your heart, and
for trusting the guidance within. Together we can celebrate
life and the journey back to our true selves. Your dedication
to living a life with more joy and love is a beautiful gift to
yourself and the world.

Also for Tucker,
I love you so much. Thank you.

The Self-Love Experiment
Resources

THE SELF-LOVE EXPERIMENT IS my own personal journey into finding self-love. Throughout this book, I share my story to help you learn by example. But there are many tools I use in my own life and in workshops and coaching sessions with my clients to help them access self-love. I'm committed to doing all I can to support you on your self-love journey, which is why I have created extra resources to help you feel more joy and self-love. This book is one tool among many to help you fall in love with yourself and life.

These powerful tools are designed to help you feel supported and loved while you read this book and create your own Self-Love Experiment.

FREE "ME MATTERS" AUDIO MEDITATION

I created a powerful audio meditation that you can download for *free* to help you align with your best self daily. This meditation will help you feel more balanced and loved. Download the free self-love audio meditation here: www.playwiththeworld.com/theselflove experiment/mematters.

COMMUNITY—FACEBOOK GROUP

I've created a tight-knit, collaborative community on my Facebook author page at @ShannonKaiserWrites. This is a community where I post tools, resources, and daily inspiration. This is a safe place for readers to connect. Share your reflections, your questions, and your brilliant "aha" moments.

SELF-LOVE POWER MANTRAS

Throughout the book you will see key phrases and positive mantras. Each on its own page, these are designed to be used as motivation. You can snap a pic, post to social media, send to your friends, or simply copy them and put them on your own vision board. You can use them to help you feel connected to your authentic self.

SHARE THE LOVE #THESELFLOVEEXPERIMENT

When you are inspired by messages and mantras in this book, share them on social media using #TheSelfLoveExperiment or #MeMatters. I invite you to take photos of the book cover or any text that inspires you and post to your Instagram page, as I am always reposting readers' photos. Just make sure to use the hashtags #TheSelfLoveExperiment or #MeMatters or tag @Shannon KaiserWrites so I can find you.

JOY JOURNAL—POWER QUESTIONS

Throughout the book I ask specific questions to help you take the process deeper. I encourage you to get a special journal for the process and have fun answering the questions, strategically designed for maximum growth.

SELF-LOVE SOUNDTRACK

Get sweet music for your ears by listening to the free soundtrack I created of uplifting songs I use in my Self-Love workshops and in-person events. You can access the free playlist on www.play withtheworld.com/theselfloveexperiment.

Contents

PART 1

BEAUTY IN BREAKDOWN
There Is Purpose to the Pain

PART 2

THE SELF-LOVE EXPERIMENT

PART 6

THE SELF-LOVE PRINCIPLES

Download the Free Self-Love
"Me Matters" Audio Meditation

www.playwiththeworld.com/
theselfloveexperiment/mematters

To be nobody but yourself—in a world which is doing
its best, night and day, to make you everybody else—
means to fight the hardest battle which any human
being can fight; and never stop fighting.

—E. E. CUMMINGS

Why This Book?
Why Now?

I HAVE WHAT I refer to as a guru. But he is also my life coach, adviser, and healer. The term doesn't really matter, as he has been all these things and more for me, and I am eternally grateful to him for having helped me sort through some very difficult life situations. For the sake of protecting his privacy, we shall call him Doctor P. The last time I met with him, he told me, "You will find lasting love when you love yourself. Your only homework is to Love Yourself." I felt like a helpless child watching as an adult dangled candy in front of me. The sweet thing I wanted so badly in my life was right there in front of me yet completely out of my reach. His words echoed in my mind: "All you have to do is love yourself and you will have everything you want."

Sigh.

I thought to myself, "I am trying. I've been trying. But when will it get easier?" You see, at the time I met with my guru, I was about to embark on an inward journey. I had already been focusing on knowing that me matters. But it was fleeting. Some days I felt great, I enjoyed my own company, and I liked who I was, but most days I felt unworthy, ugly, and off track in life.

Welcome to the Self-Love Experiment.

What is it, you might ask? The Self-Love Experiment is a challenge I gave myself to become my own best friend. It was born out of a desperate need to feel more connected to my life and myself. I wanted to know what it was like to live at peace with myself in my body and finally end the war I had been carrying on inside myself for more than three decades. Was it possible that this battle might finally subside? I wanted to find out, so I set out on a giant adventure. The Self-Love Experiment is a love story. Not the kind where a Prince Charming comes to rescue you from distress, but the kind of love story where you become your own hero. I rose up and learned how to save myself from the demons that live in my head. Before my Self-Love Experiment, self-criticism formed the backbone of my relationship with myself. I was always attacking myself in my mind, overanalyzing everything I did. Nothing I ever did was good enough for me.

I wanted to know what it would feel like to go an entire day without criticizing myself or feeling as though I didn't measure up. "Heck," I thought, "it would be nice to go even an hour without this inner critic beating me down." So I set out to work on myself, for myself, and by myself.

For more than three decades, I didn't just dislike myself—I actively went out of my way to sabotage myself. Although I didn't know it at the time, I was indeed treating myself like dirt. All through my twenties I picked inappropriate men who were not right for me in myriad ways: drug addicts, unavailable men, or men who were super clingy and liked the idea of me rather than who I really was. All my relationships were superficial. I overspent, overate, overworked, all in an effort to avoid the sinking sensation that perhaps there might be a gentler, kinder, and more compassionate way to live.

Was it possible to love myself? When I looked around at my circle of friends and family and in society, it became obvious that most people don't really love themselves. It's not that we don't want to. We just don't know how. And most of us aren't talking about it. We aren't walking around saying we don't love ourselves; rather, it's in our behavior, our way of existing. It's in our constant quest to be happier, skinnier, smarter, and richer—outward expressions of achievement that we reach for, based on some notion that we just aren't enough as we are. We try and we try to be enough. It is fleeting, the sensation of getting there. The chase is what we are conditioned to accept.

In doing research I discovered:[1]

- ✳ 91 percent of women *hate* their bodies.
- ✳ 89 percent of women are always on a diet or trying to lose weight.
- ✳ Twice as many American women than men are on antidepressants.
- ✳ 95 percent of people want to change something about themselves.
- ✳ People today are less happy than in the 1970s (and women then had even fewer opportunities and less freedom).
- ✳ Studies estimate ten million women and girls suffer from eating disorders as a way to control their out-of-control lives.
- ✳ Eating disorders have the highest mortality rate of any mental illness.

But it's not just women who are seemingly unable to love themselves. It's men, too. And who is the culprit? It's that mean part of us that says we aren't worthy or lovable. The inner critic that creates a playground for our lack of self-love. It is the judgmental, critical, and belittling inner dialogue that virtually every person hears running through their mind every day.

It became clear that, in order for me to find self-love, I had to look at what was blocking me, which was my own inner critic and the beliefs about myself and how others perceived me. It is the part of me that tried to sabotage my efforts at being happy. It is the inner voice that points out all the ways we don't measure up or might be falling behind . . . how fat, old, young, uneducated, or flawed we are. The part of us that says we should be doing more, we should have it figured out. The voice that says we are off track and therefore doomed. For most of us, this voice is very much in the driver's seat, making it highly unlikely that we will ever reach the destination of self-love. We worry we are "not enough" or we are being "too much." We judge ourselves for just existing. We focus on what is not going well and how far we still have to go instead of celebrating the journey and appreciating where we are, as we are.

Self-love is not something that comes naturally to adults or something we actually think about trying to achieve. Many of us, it seems, search for happiness and fulfillment, and we think this will give us the feeling of peace we have so long desired. But we quickly learn that happiness and even being fulfilled are constantly moving targets.

I wanted to know what it felt like to fall in love with myself. "Falling" was an important part of my process, because falling in love is an essential first part of loving someone for a long, long time and loving them unconditionally. When we fall in love in romantic relationships, everything is heightened, and we are diligent in our devotion to our beloved. We are excited about the possibilities of what might be, and we allow ourselves to be present to what is. In our fascination with this person we don't see any of their flaws. I wanted to feel all of this about myself, but I knew that—just like real romance—the falling is fleeting, and at some point we must roll up our sleeves and get down to the hard work of making love last.

This full circle of self-love—falling in love with yourself and then discovering how to make that love last—is essential. And it's a process that is so very rewarding because suddenly we find that we have discovered a gentler, kinder way to live in the world. One where we are no longer at war with ourselves but are simply celebrating ourselves in a loving light. Imagine what it would feel like to live your life at ease, never feeling the pressure to change or fix yourself. No more pressure to be different so you fit in or feel accepted, because you know you are enough. I believe that this way of living is entirely possible, which is what this book is about.

Thus began my Self-Love Experiment. I first started by asking myself, "How do people love themselves? What tools and tips can I try?" I tried meditation. I tried repeating self-acceptance mantras. I looked in the mirror and tried to compliment myself several times each day. I read tons of self-help books and experimented with even more diets. I took all kinds of steps, but all my efforts were strained. Something was still off. I still felt unlovable, like an outsider looking in on my life. Not fully feeling as though I belonged anywhere. The big question echoed in my mind: How do I love myself?

If only I knew *how,* I could take the steps necessary and make it happen. But asking *how* when we don't know how just keeps us stuck. So I stopped asking *how* do you love yourself, and I started to experiment. The first step: I began to ask better questions.

Perhaps the better question to start with is *why*? Why don't I love myself? The answer was unclear at first. I liked parts of me, but when it came to actually committing to loving myself, I felt a little unsure. I just knew that I felt, for some reason, unworthy. Where it started, this insecure way of being, was unclear. And perhaps it didn't really matter—all I knew was that I wanted to feel something about myself that just didn't come naturally to me.

In order to fall in love with myself, I needed a fresh start, a clean slate. No more regrets about the past. I thought about the moments when I did appreciate myself and felt excited about life. But then I thought about how, following these brief moments of self-appreciation, I would find myself looking in the mirror and hearing my inner voice interrupt my good vibes with self-doubt and judgments as I compared myself to others and concluded that I just didn't measure up. It seemed every time I managed to see myself in a positive light, my harsh inner critic interrupted the reverie to assert that, No, actually you just aren't good enough.

But why exactly didn't I love me?

I thought, "Well, let's start there." Before my experiment, I felt unlovable. I didn't love me . . . why? Because I was fat and overweight. How can an overweight person be loved? Because I felt ugly, I never felt like I fit in, I've always felt like I'm on the outside looking in, one of the uncool kids trying to prove myself worthy. Why don't I love myself? Because I don't always feel smart. I don't always know the right thing to say, I often forget things, and I am clumsy with details. Because I feel like maybe my life is off track. Maybe somehow I took a wrong turn and I'm behind, I'm not where I'm supposed to be. I make mistakes, and everything is always my fault. Because I feel like I don't matter. Like I have nothing of real value to offer others. Because I am alone. A single woman in her midthirties . . . surely something is wrong with me.

There it was, scratched out on my notepad, all the reasons I felt ashamed to be alive. The reasons staring me in the face: proof that I was unworthy. As I looked at my list, I saw a consistency with its focus on my feeling a certain way—not good enough, not lovable. These clues into my deep-rooted insecurity were like bread crumbs leading me through a thicket of limiting beliefs about myself.

I dug a little deeper. My entire life I felt ashamed to be me. I felt unworthy of being alive in the world. This way of living no longer served me. This way of being had to die. It was time for me to shed the cloak of fear and rise up to see my beautiful essence and know that I am worthy of love, acceptance, recognition, and joy. All I had to do was just decide. Because feeling as though we don't have a choice is indeed a choice. We deserve to love ourselves. By recognizing this, I felt a little freer. And the choice to be kinder to me was under way.

Before my Self-Love Experiment, my biggest fear—that I wouldn't be accepted for who I was—was because I didn't accept myself as I was. And although I was unaware of it at the time, I was still needing the approval of others. Ironically, I wanted to be seen for who I was, but I was at the same time terrified of being seen. I'd think, What if people don't like me? What if others laugh at me for being who I really am? I realized the only way to see if self-love was possible was to start taking action and exploring the possibilities of what might be. It was important to allow myself to be more me.

How? What does this mean? Simply put, we will try. We will be willing. We will open ourselves up a little more to the possibilities of self-love. The Self-Love Experiment involves agreeing in your heart and in your actions to the following new ways of being in the world:

* I made a declaration to myself, that I will simply show up.
* I will speak kindly to myself, no more criticism.
* I will stop judging myself, no more comparing.
* I will stop feeling guilty for just doing things I really want to do.
* I will stop blaming myself and feeling as though it's always my fault.
* I will start to care for myself in ways that cherish and appreciate my being.
* I will show up for myself.

* I will trust myself.
* I will no longer avoid my feelings.
* I will express myself and say what I need to say.
* I will let go of the habits, fears, and beliefs blocking
  me from feeling content with myself.

Boiled down and at its essence, the Self-Love Experiment begins when you commit to learning how to exist in this world alongside the inner critic that has raged war on you for possibly even decades of your life. It means learning to love the unlovable parts of yourself. When I committed to doing my own Self-Love Experiment, I told myself that I would allow myself to be who I am instead of who I think I am supposed to be or who the world says I should be.

How do you love yourself? What we are really asking is, How can you love something you think is unlovable? You try. We just have to simply show up, roll up our sleeves, and try. In this way, one day at a time, the Self-Love Experiment will unfold. And it will be the most beautiful journey you will ever embark on. Welcome to the adventure of becoming your own best friend.

It's hard to love yourself

when you're not being yourself.

–TONY ROBBINS

Introduction

I AM NOT A technical or scientific person. I love research and researchers and all that they do, but I am a feeling person. I learn from my life experiences, my mistakes, and my feelings. They lead me forward and help me figure things out. This book is not a technical or scientific approach to reaching self-love. Rather, it describes my own personal journey to discover that I matter and that self-love is indeed possible. In my sharing, I hope you can learn through example. I will share my story, and in my sharing, you can apply the aspects that resonate with you for your own life. I might be talking about my insecurities and how I overcame them, and my hang-ups might not be yours, but if you apply your hang-ups to the experiment, you will see results for yourself, too. The goal is to become our own friends, even if we all have a different point of entry. You may not hate your body as I did, but you might hate something else that you think is holding you back. Just be open to the journey, and you, too, will see a shift in your own life.

With that said, as I wrote the first few drafts of this book, I kept wanting to put the self-love into a process. It made sense to me to have steps. After all, if we take the steps, we should be able to see results, right? Technically this is correct, but draft after draft, the book kept feeling like it wanted to be something else. It felt incomplete. It wanted to be more organic, less formal, and not so technical. About the time I got the original idea to write this book, I was reading Gretchen Rubin's *Better Than Before*,[2] an instant *New York Times* bestseller. Her book is all about transforming habits, and her approach is very linear. She indeed has mastered the step-by-step process; it is approachable, simple, and applicable. I started to look at other authors to see if there was a secret to their success and any one-size-fits-all approach to self-improvement and laying out a book. The more I compared my approach to that of other authors, the more overwhelmed and anxious I became.

2

> It never occurred to me that trying to change my outside world was a desperate attempt to feel better on the inside.

I kept trying to put my book into a formula, a specific structure, one I thought worked because it seemed to work for other authors. I thought if it worked for them—the formatting, the approach, even the structure—then it should work for me. I tried to shove my understanding of self-love into a cookie-cutter version of what was established. Little did I know at the time, but that was how my entire life was functioning. I was always trying to shove myself into situations that didn't really align or fit. I'd do what others wanted, not really giving myself a chance to speak up or do what I wanted. I wanted to fit in, but I was always a little off. I was trying to fit into the world, but as long as I kept trying to fit, I would always come up short, because the real magic of the Self-Love Experiment is that I learned I don't have to fit into the world. I can be me and let the world fit to me. There is no need to change ourselves to be something else, because we, as we are, are enough.

Most of my life was focused on trying to change myself on the outside. I was always trying to fit my body to a certain size, trying to say the right thing and hide my real opinion, afraid to rock any boat. I was always trying to manipulate, control, or change situations, circumstances, and myself.

I walked around an anxious ball of frustration. I was in a perpetual state of fear. I always felt as if I had to gasp for air. I was alive but barely living.

My anxiety got so bad at times that I would forget to breathe and I would pass out. This is all because I was working so hard to change myself, to change my life, but I didn't have self-love. I didn't even know what self-love was.

My shift came after writing multiple drafts of this book. Through my own Self-Love Experiment, I stopped trying to push and make myself be something I am not. I gave myself permission to be me. The same thing happened through the process of writing this book. Instead of trying to make it something it wasn't supposed to be, I decided to let go of the rules and formulas of reaching self-love. I stopped comparing myself to other authors and just let the book and me be what we wanted to be: free to express itself, free to just be me.

Once I let go of trying to make this book something it wasn't, I was able to invite the real me to the adventure. The real me does not have a clear step-by-step process of reaching self-love, but she has stories, adventures, ideas, thoughts, and a deep understanding that spawns from personal experience, all of which I have a deep desire to share.

So I put them into this book to document my own journey into finding self-love. What you will find are stories and ideas, and as I

3

share my perspective, I invite you to learn by my example. My other books have been more prescriptive; I provided more checklists and questions to help you deep dive into your own life. This book is much different. Why? Because self-love is a very personal experience. This is my own personal journey into finding my authentic self, and not only finding her but also loving her unconditionally and realizing there is nothing to change or fix. You may be wondering why this is important. Because you too are on your own personal journey. By picking up this book you've already declared you are ready to love yourself more. I am enough. You are enough. We are enough.

4

> There is a power in sharing; when we share our true, real, raw selves with others, we can celebrate all that we are.

This book is a journey, just like life and just like discovering self-love. If you are looking for the answers and you want your magic bullet, if you want some expert to tell you exactly how to find self-love, I'll be honest: this book and my teachings are not for you. What I offer is my truth, a reflective process that is full of love, compassion, and wonder. I tend to learn best through example, and personally I like stories, as they can touch us in ways that move us to action. So here in these pages are hundreds of stories, examples, and insights into what self-love is and how to reach it. Take what works for you, leave the rest, but please, dear friend, have fun in this experiment and be open in the journey.

I share my examples and learning because what I have been through and learned is nothing short of miraculous. I've discovered the power of being your own best friend, and in sharing my story, I hope you find a peace within. Please remember this is an experiment, which means the outcome is not as important as the journey. As long as you approach this book with an open heart, you will get so much more out of it than if you are trying to find the answer and looking to be fixed. Because it is an experiment, with this approach you will see there is nothing to fix. What I learned through my own journey is that there are only areas of our life and pieces to be loved. So any area that feels out of balance and is not going as well as you hope is neither broken nor in need of change for you to be happy. It just needs a little more love.

What I learned is that self-love is not an organized process or even a destination.

Self-love is not a place we get to but a place we choose.

Specific steps and practical tools are good, but life doesn't work that way. Real life, like my experiment to find self-love, is messy, gloriously raw, and exciting. There are no parameters or regulations. It doesn't fit neatly into a box. It's about the journey, the story that unfolds with each new discovery. All you have to do is be open and suck in the experience, because life will give you what you need, when you ask for it.

I set out to find self-love. And I found it. Today, I love me. I feel peace. I realized the steps can be practical, but self-love is not. Finding self-love has to happen from within our own hearts. Yes, there are action steps you can take, the principles I share in the final section, but relying on only the steps will inevitably keep you missing the real magic of possibilities that can happen when we take off the blinders.

I applied the principles to my life, but I applied them loosely, and as I loosened the reins, I felt freer. In the space of freedom, I was able to be more me. And that is what this entire process is really about: letting yourself be more you, instead of you trying to be more of what you think you need to be. That is the power of the experiment. And in the process of just being you, freedom can come in, and love and joy will commence.

I feel as though I should share that this is the fifth draft of this book. Yes, that is correct: I wrote four other versions of *The Self-Love Experiment*. For a couple of reasons, really. One, I don't like to put anything out into the world unless I am super proud of it and connected to the message, and two, I need to believe in what I am writing about. And for the past year, I have been trying to see the results before the experiment was over. I wanted to feel self-love; for a while the destination was more important than the journey. "I have a book to write," I told myself, "so put this process on paper." But that approach was putting the cart before the horse. It wasn't flowing. Nothing was working. It even took almost six months to finalize the contract for this book with my publisher; the entire process was molasses slow, which begged for self-compassion. The more gentle I was with myself, the easier things became. The more I let go of the destination, the more fun my experiment was.

You see, I am actually living daily what I'm writing about. I indeed have been on a journey, a true self-love experiment. Five drafts ago, I had an entirely different relationship with myself—and it wasn't as good as the one I have with myself now! As I dive more deeply into my own Self-Love Experiment, I learn more and grow into even more self-awareness. In this experience, I learned we are always right where we need to be. Check in with yourself and see where you are today. How do you feel? What is your relationship with yourself? Knowing where you are today is key to getting where you want to go. I had to go through all those experiences and book drafts to learn the lessons and love myself fully. Every step of the way is a process, so please be compassionate and kind with yourself, for wherever you are is exactly where you are supposed to be.

This book is not like my others. I mean, it's still me, I am the author, but I feel as though this particular book, because of the nature of the topic, has asked me to go deeper, step up higher, and demand more from myself, my writing, and my audience. What do I mean? I mean the Self-Love Experiment is more than just an experiment—it is a declaration of sorts to your future self. You are saying you will show up more fully and be more present for yourself. You will be the best version of you because you know you are worth it. Well, at least that is what the Self-Love Experiment was for me.

In the first few drafts, every word made me excruciatingly uncomfortable. I felt as though I were climbing a mountain every day I showed up to write the book. It was uncomfortable. I felt naked and exposed, like that bad reoccurring dream where you are naked in public. Only in my dream, no one was laughing. They just stared at me as though I were some social leper; they pointed and whispered under their breaths. It seemed as if they were one collective unit and I was on the outside, always looking in, much like a zoo animal that feels trapped by life's circumstances. I felt judgment, shame, and oh so out of place. That is my dream, but that was also my life. No, I didn't walk around naked in public, and I am not really trapped behind bars, but that's what I felt like for much of the process of documenting my experience. I felt out of place. I felt like I didn't belong, and perhaps we have to start there, because self-love isn't just about becoming your own best friend. It is layered. And one layer is acceptance, feeling as if you fit when otherwise you often don't. If there is an area of your life that "doesn't fit," self-love gives it permission to fit.

There are many layers, and I did show up for this book, as hard and uncomfortable as it was for me to write. I showed up because that is the whole point. Dear friend, that is the only point to self-

7

love. Showing up. This book and the process to bring it forth are a metaphor for the journey to actualizing ourselves into self-acceptance and love. For me, this book had to be written despite the uncomfortable feelings and painful perseverance. I not only showed up but I also had to push past my comfort levels. And that is the entire bedrock of the Self-Love Experiment: to push past what we know in order to experience breakthroughs.

We can't reach new heights if we stay comfortable. We have to be willing to go beyond what we know in order to see new results. I was too comfortable. I was settling. I was living my life but not fully alive. I was stuck in a routine; I felt alone, empty, and bored with life. It wasn't just that I didn't love myself, but I also wasn't connected by my own life. For most of us, everything is a routine, and we get too comfortable. This book is indeed my own Self-Love Experiment, but it isn't about me, really. I mean, it is, but it is more about you and the world and how we are all really very similar. No matter who we are, where we come from, what we do, or where we live in the world, we are more similar than we realize. Because at the core of our insecurities, frustrations, and pain is the need to be loved, to give love, and to want to be appreciated and seen for who we really are. But how can we really do that if we don't know who we are? This book is my journey into my own heart to discover that everything I ever needed was never out there. It was in here, in my heart, in my soul. In recognition of self, we can shine.

So, yes, I will be telling you my story, but it is *our* story. You are here and reading this for a reason. The experiment is ours together. As far as the book writing, the process to get this book out into the world was not natural. The same way self-love, at first, feels so unnatural, so was every phase of writing this book. But when you keep at it, and believe in it, it will happen for you. Remember, self-love is a process. And the most important part is just showing up. By holding this book in your hands, you are showing up.

Draft one was all about weight loss. I thought if I lost weight, I would feel self-love. I lost some weight, and some of it came back. And I realized self-love has nothing to do with how you look but everything to do with how you live. Onward to draft two.

Draft two was all about the sutras. These are clear, actionable steps to self-love, and when you apply them to your life, voilà! You have arrived into a loving utopia of happily ever after. I didn't even finish that draft because it was clear early on that there are no clear sutras or laws to falling in love with yourself. It is not black-and-white, nor is there a cookie-cutter process. Next.

Draft three was all about steps. Okay, no laws or sutras, but now I'll list clear steps. We can apply the steps to our lives, and when we take the steps we will see results. Like working out, if you are consistent, you will become stronger and see results. Well, this step-by-step process was failing me. I felt further from self-love than ever. So I sat down and started draft four.

Draft four, the stages of love. When we fall in love with another person, there are stages. What if I applied those stages to my own self? Bingo! We might be on to something.

1. The Romance Stage
2. The Power-Struggle Stage
3. The Stability Stage
4. The Commitment Stage
5. The Cocreation or Bliss Stage

I first took baths and even treated myself to fancy spa treatments. Then I tried to be more powerful by owning my worth, speaking my truth, and expressing myself more. But bliss never came. It did for moments, but it never really stayed for long. I realized very soon that I was trying too hard. I was trying to make my experiment work, and I was focused on the outcome. The result was my obsession. I thought, "Will I ever reach self-love? Will I meet my soul mate? Will I lose weight? Will I fall in love with my life?"

And trying to put all my experiments into a "process" was not working. After all, falling in love with another person is different for everyone—for some, it happens at first sight; for others, it takes weeks, months, even years. I was on the decades plan. It took me what felt like a lifetime to fall in love with myself, but I kept showing up, and my dedication and loyalty paid off. I kept saying, "At least I am trying." I thought about all the times I've fallen in love with romantic partners. Every single relationship was totally different. Sometimes it happened fast, and I knew within seconds of meeting that person; other times it took months, in some cases years, for me to realize I loved someone. You just have to trust your heart. Knowing this, I realized that my heart was not leading my experiment. I needed to add more heart and let it be. You can't force love. You can only try. It became clear to me that my relationship was more like an arranged marriage. I was in a body that I didn't like, and this was something I had to live with. Much like an arranged marriage, we don't have much choice. We just have to accept it. We can do the best we can to find the love within the unlovable, but it is our responsibility to make the most of it. It always comes back to acceptance. It seems the first place we must dive into is self-acceptance.

What you hold in your hand is a real-life love story. One with infatuation, understanding, concern, trepidation, lust, fear, doubt, joy, and clarity.

Like any good love story, there is depth; there is magic and a little bit of drama, but the happy ending is not part of this story. For this story is more important than the result. And the happiness is in the story itself.

Welcome to my Self-Love Experiment. My real-life love story.

I remember when I thought

things were so hard and I would

never make it through, I thought

I would never recover. And today

I smile. I smile because I am truly

proud of myself. I am proud of

the person I have fought

to become.

—ANONYMOUS

PART 1

BEAUTY IN BREAKDOWN

There Is Purpose to the Pain

Difficult Roads Lead to Divine Destinations

TODAY I AM COMMITTED to caring for myself. I can look in the mirror and smile in gratitude for who I am and how far I've come. I can truly say, "I love myself." But it hasn't always been this way. I spent more than three decades at war with myself. I hated my body; it was to blame for everything in my life. The failed relationships, the missed opportunities, the rejection and ridicule—it was my body's entire fault, or so I thought.

For years I would pinch my extra skin, cry out into the dark night, praying for a thinner body, a different frame, a smaller stomach. I hated myself because I despised the way I looked. The majority of my thoughts were obsessive about how large, ugly, or unworthy I was. I couldn't look into mirrors without saying hateful words about how I felt. I thought my life would be better when I was "not me" but smaller, thinner, not so chubby, not thick or round. I wanted to change so badly, but every failed diet resulted in lower self-esteem, more guilt, and even more self-sabotage. Even when the diets worked (for a short period), when I lost all the weight, I still hated me. I thought I needed my body to change in order for me to have a happy life. But when it changed, my inner critic never did. I'd lose ten pounds and gain twenty. This continued for two full decades until I found myself almost a hundred pounds overweight and experiencing a complete disappearing act of self-esteem.

I found myself crying in a hotel bathroom, ashamed to look in the mirror. I was hours away from going on a Seattle morning television show to talk about my first book and share tips on how to be happy. I was teaching others how to be happy, but I couldn't find one good thing to say about myself. That was the moment when I realized something needed to change.

Sure, I was happier than I had ever been. A few years prior I had just barely made it through some major life changes. I left my corporate job in advertising, moved across the country, left a man who wanted to marry me, and overcame eating disorders, drug addiction, and clinical depression to follow my heart and become a writer. Here I was, living my dream life, but it still felt like a dream. I didn't recognize my body, or who I was. I wasn't fully in love with my life because I didn't love all of me; I didn't think I mattered. I spent so many years trying to help and be there for other people that I had sacrificed myself. My needs were never met. I wasn't living to my fullest because I still hated my body.

It was at that moment, when looking into the hotel mirror, that I made a promise to myself. I said, "Shannon, your full-time mission is to find self-love. It's time to become your own best friend."

Over the next few years I went on a deep inward journey, what I call the Self-Love Experiment, and I discovered the most beautiful thing in the world: Me Matters.

Me Matters is an acceptance of self and knowing that you are perfect as you are, for the imperfections are what make us beautiful. It is years of trial and error, books, courses, and personal exploration refined and tuned into a solid guide, the fifteen principles to true self-acceptance and love.

The miracle came not in my body changing but in the change in my heart. I looked in the mirror and said, "I am committed to you. I am going to learn how to love you."

And in finding love for self, everything changed.

This book is the result of my exploration, which I use in my life and in my own personal coaching practice. Hundreds of clients and tens of thousands of readers worldwide have used these tools to help them be more compassionate with themselves and learn how to trust their own inner guidance. When you trust yourself, you make better choices. But in order to trust yourself, you need love.

After going through the Self-Love Experiment, I could finally accept myself for who I was, as I was. Learning how to love me has been the most difficult thing I have ever had to do. Not because loving yourself is particularly hard, but because I had to unlearn all of the things I was conditioned to believe about self-love: I can't love myself because it is selfish. I am not good enough unless I am a smaller size. I don't belong unless I lose weight. That I can't have what I want, or be successful, or be accepted, or be regarded as attractive if I am overweight. I believed I couldn't love myself if I had weight to lose.

The thing is, I would lose that weight and nothing would change. On the outside, people praised me, complimented me. I was treated much differently, sure, but on the inside, I still disliked me, I still avoided mirrors. Weight was never the problem. I was still at war with myself within my own head. The battle persisted for thirty-plus years. Until I discovered the Self-Love Experiment, a revolutionary approach that I created out of a personal need to end the madness and discover a more compassionate way to live. I use to say things like "I will be a TED Talk speaker when I lose the weight," "I will travel the world when I drop fifteen more pounds," "I will start dating again when I lose thirty pounds." These "when I's" kept me from living my life in the moment. They kept me on the outside of my potential. It wasn't until I committed to me, through the

Self-Love Experiment, that I discovered what self-love is: inner peace.

Today I love myself. I know how hard it is to live a life where you are at war with yourself. I know it can be hard to believe you are worthy of love and acceptance. I, too, once thought self-love was selfish, and I spent years avoiding my heart's desires because I didn't think my dreams mattered. All that changed when I discovered real self-acceptance. The Self-Love Experiment is about learning how to trust and love yourself. I retrained my brain to focus on loving me instead of condemning me. One step at a time I transformed my relationship with my self. It started with a desire to change. That spun from learning how to care for myself with compassion, which led to finding self-respect. In one of my favorite books, *Living with Joy* by Sanaya Roman, Sanaya writes about self-respect and knowing your worth:

What is required to feel good about yourself is not the same from person to person. What you require for self-esteem is not necessarily what another person requires. It is important to discover what makes you feel worthy, confident, and happy about who you are.

Self-respect at the highest levels comes from honoring your soul. This means speaking and acting from a level of integrity and honesty that reflects your higher self.[3]

Self-respect means coming from your power, not your weakness.

For most of my life I related to the world through my weaknesses. I felt ugly and overweight, so naturally I projected that out into the world. Learning how to love myself started with identifying my own set of beliefs about myself and removing ones that didn't serve me. I know personal development is not one-size-fits-all, which is why this book isn't going to tell you how to love yourself, lose weight, get out of debt, or find your soul mate. Instead, I will give you tools you can apply to your life to make the most out of your life. And when you do this, what you want comes to you. My approach is much different. Why? Because if we want new results, we need to approach things differently. Because you've most likely tried the courses, gym memberships, diets, and books that say this is the way, and maybe it worked for a while, but you fell back into old patterns, beliefs, and habits that didn't align with your true self. Maybe you've tried to be kinder to yourself, and maybe it worked for a little while, but you want it to stick. Like real romantic love, falling in love with you is not a one-size-fits-all approach; sometimes it is fast and easy. Other times it is slow and steady.

Love demands nothing but waits for our acceptance.

I learned we first have to learn how to trust ourselves. This book is a road map and guide to being true to you, because with self-trust everything else can flourish. When you learn to identify your own value system and align with your own truth, you can stand proud in who you are and make choices with confidence and clarity. Most of us don't have a solid relationship with ourselves, so we lean on others for approval; we try to mask our insecurities with overdoing, over–working out, overspending, overeating, and at the end of the day we feel exhausted and tired. We don't have the energy to take care of ourselves, so we settle. We settle into bigger bodies, lower bank accounts, unhealthy relationships, lost dreams yet to be manifested, and we get comfortable being uncomfortable. This becomes our regular way of life.

The Self-Love Experiment serves to reverse this. Because deep within all of us is an inner drive to rise up and show the world that we really are magnificently beautiful in all our natural glory. You don't have to change yourself to fit in; the Self-Love Experiment is a revolutionary process to give you permission to be who you are, as you are. Imagine ending the endless battle against yourself, the little voice that says, "You messed up, you aren't where you are supposed to be, you don't belong, you are never going to figure it out, you might as well give up." It's time to let that little voice go. It's time to seriously let that little voice go.

The "When Is Tomorrow Going to Be Today?" Syndrome

BEFORE I FOUND SELF-LOVE, pretty much my entire life I felt like I was waiting for my "real life" to begin. I spent the majority of my teens and early twenties trying to get out into the "real world." But once I landed my so-called dream job in advertising, it felt nothing like what I'd hoped. My doctor diagnosed me with depression, and I was suffering from eating disorders and drug addiction. I was still waiting for my "real life" to start. I longed to be a writer, but fears around letting go of all that I had worked for separated me from my "real life." Yet letting go of who I thought I needed to be in order to become who I really am was the greatest choice I ever made.

I finally got up enough courage to leave the advertising industry and find happiness free from depression, and here I sit several years later with three bestselling books and a booming business as a life coach and speaker. Yet every once in a while I still feel like my "real life" is just around the corner. I am living it, the dream life I was waiting for, yet it doesn't always feel like my life.

My professional dreams have come true for the most part—the national TV appearance hasn't happened yet, nor has Sandra

Bullock played my life story on the big screen—but I've had almost a decade of doing what I love.

That should be enough. But is it possible humans are conditioned to always strive for more? We long for tomorrows to help fulfill our todays. It's the "when is tomorrow going to be today?" syndrome. Most of us have an elusive expectation as we wait for happiness to come in; meanwhile, our life is happening now. So here I sit, living the "real life" I have been waiting so long for. When I pictured myself at this point, I imagined I'd be sitting next to Oprah, with Elizabeth Gilbert praising my latest literary wonder, on the TED Talk stage with a standing ovation at the end, and in a white dress barefoot on the beach with the love of my life.

These sweet visions still exist in my dreams. But they are not yet my reality. Is it possible our dreams distract us from reality? Here I am, living the life I spent years only dreaming about, but I can't shake the feeling that I am not quite where I think I should be. It's human to want what we don't yet have, and when we get what we want, we often skip right over the joy to keep going on to the next dream, always in pursuit of happiness. This book is about catching yourself, and instead of reaching outside of you for some far-off joy, you will learn how to cultivate a sense of self-awareness for joy in this moment. We will no longer allow our fear-based voice, the ego, to stay in the driver's seat, which is what happens when we focus on the destination more than on the journey, and we will turn our attention to the present, which invites in real happiness.

This constant quest for more, reaching for untapped dreams that live only in our hearts, burns to be realized, but before my Self-Love Experiment, it was never enough; I never felt whole. Every time we get what we want, we just turn our attention to the next big thing.

The real challenge is learning to see we are whole and complete in this moment. Just as we are sitting here right now, we are enough.

Those dreams are nice to have, but they don't make or break us. Life is the process and unfolding of glorious challenges filled with moments of inspiration. We just need to recognize this truth.

It is in the wanting and waiting that we can find balance in life.

When we get honest with ourselves, the painted version of our perfect life is often better than our reality because we imagine ourselves free of insecurities and flaws.

It's not just these experiences we aspire to have but also who we think we will become in those experiences. In our minds, most often we are worry free, thinner, smarter, richer, our problems are worked out, and we are free to just be.

Before I started writing this book, I was, admittedly, still waiting for my ideal life to begin, but the Self-Love Experiment taught me how to enjoy the journey instead of wrapping up my happiness into some goal yet to be realized. Because the truth about transformation into the unknown is inevitable but manageable.

When I sat down to write this book, it became obvious that I would have to go deep into my own patterns to teach this method and really practice it to show that it works. In order to allow happiness in, I'd have to stop chasing life and accept that this is it. I learned that wanting will never stop, but wanting the future more than today is when we fall into problems. When the wanting turns out to be waiting, we fall into the "when is tomorrow going to be today?" syndrome. When we want something that is not yet here—a bigger bank account, a smaller body, our soul mate, the dream job, etc.—it puts a focus on lack. Instead of reaching for happiness in the moment, we feel inadequate because we have yet to reach what we aspire to, hoping it will come tomorrow. This is why so many diets fail, why some people who win the lottery go bankrupt, and why divorce and depression rates are so high. It's the lack mentality that keeps us from being present or achieving lasting results. And not just the lack from falling short of our goals but also from feeling unworthy of our desires in the process.

We all have certain habits that block us from being our best self. Many are unconscious or so ingrained in our daily routine that they often hurt our success at healing. Look at every experience as an opportunity to learn and grow.

If you really want to change your life, you have to try something radically new, which I did. Instead of resisting who I was, I looked in the mirror and said, "I accept you." Instead of wishing, hoping, and praying for someone else to show up, I revised my thinking to accept what is. I chose to accept what I can't change. I looked in the mirror and said to myself, "Instead of hating you, I'm going to learn how to love you." I released the tension. I stopped the struggle.

Most of our struggle in life comes from resistance and fighting against what is.

We want to be further along, in a different body, have more money and more recognition, more of anything we don't have. This constant push keeps us just on the outside of our potential; we can never truly reach our best selves when we deny ourselves the true experience of living in each moment. People often ask me if I regret having eating disorders earlier in my life, or if I wish I never went through depression. I always respond by saying I love that part of me. I needed to experience those lessons to become who I am today. I needed to experience a plus-size body to prepare me for my future self and the lessons my soul wants and needs me to learn.

> Everything you have gone through is part of a universal assignment your soul has signed up for.

You agree to learn more about yourself by going through sometimes challenging situations. When we resist, we deny ourselves the lessons available to us. Most of us try to get through the discomfort as quickly as possible. We feel stuck and want desperately to get unstuck, but sometimes the "stuckness" is where we find results. Pema Chödrön says this beautifully:

> *In life we think the point is to pass the test or overcome the problem. The real truth is that things don't get solved. They come together for a time, and then they fall apart. Then they come together again and fall apart. It's just like that. Personal discovery and growth come from letting there be room for all of this to happen: room for grief, for sadness, for misery, for joy.*

Suffering comes from wishing things were different.

Misery is self-inflicted; when we are expecting the "idea" to overcome the "actual" or needing things (or people, or places) to be different for us so we can be happy.

*Let the hard things in life break you. Let them affect you. Let
them change you. Let these hard moments inform you. Let this
pain be your teacher. The experiences of your life are trying to
tell you something about yourself. Don't cop out on that. Don't
run away and hide under your covers. Lean into it.*

*What is this storm trying to tell you? What will you learn if
you face it with courage? With full honesty and—lean into it.*[4]

I leaned into my struggles and transformed them by allowing
them to be. Everything has its own time and place. What you are
going through right now is not your forever; you can move on from
a situation causing you distress. I approached my body size in this
same way. I decided to lean into my overweight body and accept it
by asking, "What lesson do you have for me?"

> *Dear situation I would like to change,*
> *For me, dear body,*
> *what message do you have for me?*
> *What can I learn from you?*

By asking my troubles for guidance, I was able to move past
them as being troubles. When I asked my body what message it had
for me, it clearly said, "Self-love is possible right now. You can love
yourself no matter what. I am here to show you that you are
lovable."

I did this same exercise when I was stuck in depression in my
corporate job in advertising. I asked my depression what message
it had for me. At the time I was busy trying to please everyone and
do what society thought was best for me—get a good job, meet a
man, settle down—but my depression was trying to tell me something. It wanted me to be truthful. When I asked, "Why are you
here, depression?", it responded, "You haven't been listening to

your heart." I was guided to be more honest with myself and create a life I love by doing what brings me joy. I left my corporate job and found my deep, enriching passion for writing and coaching. I found a love for life. This happened because I leaned into life and the situations causing me stress. When we stop pushing against life and lean into what is, we become more aware and focused. Our experience of life can be transformed when we step fully into the moment. Lean into it. There are great lessons to be learned.

You can apply this same technique to projects. I also asked this book what message it has for me. While writing the first few drafts I felt like I was struggling. I was struggling to try to find an answer and result before I was ready. I was struggling to live my life more purposefully, I was struggling to be thankful for the aspects of me I disliked, and everything seemed hard. So I turned to the guidance available and I asked the book "process," "What am I learning? What message do you have for me?" My inner voice chimed in, "You are learning patience, you are learning about the true magic of self-love, you are learning how to let go of how you think it is supposed to look, you are learning how to appreciate who you are, and you are learning how to show up for yourself in ways you never have before." All these key learnings became the foundation for my experiment. Finally, the real Self-Love Experiment was under way.

Suddenly it made sense:

to stop hating myself is to raise

the vibration and love on the

planet. To stop loathing myself

is to reduce the negativity and

pain in the world.

—SHANNON KAISER

THE SELF-LOVE EXPERIMENT

HAVE YOU EVER HAD a conversation that became a pivotal moment of change for you? Someone said exactly what you needed to hear at the exact right time? This happened at the beginning of my Self-Love Experiment. It all started with an innocent comment my mom made. One simple sentence that changed my focus and attention and the direction of my life. When she said it, she didn't know it was important, nor did I. But looking back, it all started there, in my parents' dining room.

I was sitting at the table with my mother and we were coloring in her garden coloring book. I was filling in a flower that had big bold words that read, "Everything Happens for a Reason." I couldn't help but think that this was a universal message glaring me in the face. We were both happy, peacefully sitting together, doing what we loved. We were talking about life and dreams, all while being creative. She started talking about family friends and their new relationships. Within seconds a fear thought brushed over me, and I started to cry. I didn't know I had tears stuck inside, but they popped to the surface fast and abruptly.

I sat there at her dining room table, consumed by my own insecurity. I couldn't hold it back any longer. I couldn't hide my fear or shame; it burst out and was begging to be seen. It needed attention so much so that it interrupted my moment of bliss and contentment. I said to my mom through my tears, "I have a serious question to ask you."

She looked up at me and put down her marker to give me her full attention. I said with hesitation, "Do you think a man can love me the way that I am?" In that small sentence, only thirteen words, lies everything you need to know about me in that moment in my life, how I was raised, and why I felt so stuck and off track. My mom immediately reacted and said, "Of course! Don't ever say that again. You are beautiful as you are." She was almost offended that her daughter could think such a thought, but this was the language of my head. For years I had saturated myself in this fear that I was somehow unworthy of love. How could someone love me the way I was? I wanted to be beautiful, sophisticated, graceful, and at ease in my body and in my life, but to me I was overweight, short, awkward, and frumpy, and that meant odd, that meant I didn't fit in.

My mom said, "Don't you ever think that about yourself . . . you have so much to offer."

But you see, at that point in my life I was at my emotional rock bottom. I had gained more than a hundred pounds since leaving my corporate job to start my own business as a writer and coach. I felt invisible to men and, really, to the entire world, and I worried I would never find someone to love me as I was. I didn't know it at the time, but what I really was asking my mom was, "Do you think I can ever love me as I am? Am I worthy of my own love and care?"

That small exchange between us was the catalyst that moved me to my soon-to-be Self-Love Experiment. I didn't know it at the time, my mom didn't know it, but my future self was guiding me.

Up until that point, I was dancing around on the surface of my potential, not really taking care of myself or showing up for me. The mention of self-love or even self-care was a foreign concept. One I could barely grasp. Up until that point in my life I had tried to become happy by reaching new goals, changing my behavior, or trying to manipulate certain aspects of my life or me, all in an effort to be more peaceful. I'd reach the goal, the new job, the new boyfriend, the new body, and I still felt like something was missing. I didn't really care about myself because my fears were blocking me.

The real work had to happen on the inside, which meant I had to get to the root cause of why I felt unlovable and unworthy. Love in any form could not come to me if this belief was shielding me.

That one night, that little conversation, changed it all for me. The reason that conversation, that night, that particular exchange was so important is because of what my mother said next. . .

My mom chimed in and said, "It doesn't matter what size you are or how you look. It's just about you being happy, and if you are not happy in your current size, that is not the right size for you." My mom was trying to help, but her words stung my heart. They stuck with me for weeks after our conversation. Because a part of me knew she was right. I really had only two choices: change what I couldn't accept, or accept what I couldn't change (as the proverb suggests). My body was what I hated, the size of it, the way it looked, and the lumpy shape. Could I really accept me? As my mother had suggested, if I couldn't accept it then I would have to change it, and then happiness and love might find me.

I was at the place of no return. I could no longer stay stuck in my insecurities. I knew I had to change. But I didn't know if changing my body was the way to happiness. I had tried that before, and it hadn't worked. What would make this time different? Then I had a novel thought: "Instead of trying to change me, why don't I just love me?"

My mother was suggesting that I change myself in order to love myself. She meant this in the kindest way possible, but here is the same woman from whom I would hide my food in the closet when I was eight years old. I'd sneak off before dinner and eat my favorite candy bar out of sight, because to her sugar was bad and unhealthful. The problem: I loved it. You can see the dilemma for a little girl who wants to please her mom. I was always in direct conflict with her, if unspoken, as I wanted my mom to be proud of me and love me, so I hid what I loved, sweet treats, from her. At a young age I learned that to be accepted I had to hide my true feelings and desires. I had to stuff them away or do what I really wanted in private away from others.

You may see the fallacy in this, but this is exactly what happens. We all have learned behaviors from our childhood. You may not have hidden in the closet, eating your favorite foods, but maybe you did hide a part of yourself at a young age. What happens is we do something that we think is natural to us—eating candy was natural and fun for me—but the world, our parents, society, even our inner critic comes in and says, "What you think is good is really bad." We interpret this as: we are bad for liking the things we like. We put so much pressure on ourselves to fit in and be liked that we forget to bring ourselves along for the journey.

At a young age I thought I couldn't be who I was and be accepted, so I pretended that who I really was, the chubby little girl who liked sugar, wasn't really that girl. In order for me to feel accepted, I denied myself the things I really wanted, which, as you can imagine, caused desperation, pain, and internal angst.

This pattern of denying myself, my true desires, resulted in my crying in front of my mother as an adult. I was ashamed of myself because I never allowed myself to be who I really was. Maybe the reason I wasn't able to love myself was because I was trying so hard to be someone else so I could fit into the world. Maybe the fix was to just be more of me, let me be my true self.

My mom was unaware, but her comment was simply probing me to change if I wanted to be happy. I have to change. But my own heart wanted to find self-love with the way I was in that moment. I had spent my entire life trying to change, trying to fit in, and that clearly wasn't working out for me. That way of being caused depression, eating disorders, and addictions. I needed something different. Truth be told, as long as I was confiding in other people, I could never make headway. It was time to explore my own rhythms and natural tendencies. Time to eliminate the outward chatter and start to listen to my own needs. This idea percolated for a few weeks until I realized I must dive deeper. Now the Self-Love Experiment was alive and kicking.

My entry point to self-love was my lack of body care and lack of body love. My body needed me. I may not have fully grasped the idea of body love in that moment, but this body needed my love. My body was, at that time, larger than life, but that in itself was my body screaming out to be seen, to be cared for, and to be loved. This body that craved attention and needed love was crying out because it wanted to be desired, but the body I was in was ignored, bumped into, could barely fit into airplane seats, judged, and criticized for being lazy and unmotivated. That was the house I lived in. That was the body I needed to learn how to love. Could I love seemingly unlovable parts of me?

This story is not about my body—well, yes, it is about "the body" because I live in this vehicle, and in order for me to fully reach self-love I must accept all aspects of myself, no matter how they seem. They are in my life for a reason. We are here to learn from our insecurities, but looking at the bigger picture, this Self-Love Experiment is about going headfirst into our insecurities and biggest pain points and suffering. For me, it was my relationship with my body. For you, it may be your relationship status or lack thereof, the fact that you may feel off track or behind, or maybe you, too, hate a part of yourself or your physical appearance. If you ever say, "I need to change x, y, z," or "I need to 'fix' a, b, or c," or "I need to address this part of me," then you, too, can apply the Self-Love Experiment to your life. Because needing to change, fix, or manipulate any area of our lives in an effort to reach something we don't currently have, such as happiness, peace, and love, is the fastest

35

way to stay stuck. It keeps you in the chase. It's like a handsome, alluring playboy—addicted to the intoxicating charm, the drama of desire. The chase craves opportunity; once the chase captures, he disappears, leaving you cold, ashamed, and even lonelier. The chase never ends well. And the chase never reaches its destination; it is simply the chase that is the chase's reward. This means we are stuck in the chase, conditioned to always try to reach for more than what is. This is really our drug of choice. This is the obsession we secretly cling to.

36

Naturally, in order for me to remove myself from the hectic hamster wheel of chasing the elusive there, I had to look at my habits and start with self-care.

I was never the most confident person. When I was young, we moved around a lot, so as the new kid I was picked on quite a bit. As children we never know the outcome of experiences gone bad, which results in decades of insecurity, loneliness, and shame. As children we just go through the experiences, but each one presses into our psyche and teaches us how to react and interact in the world. Each experience becomes a teacher, showing us what to do and what not to do.

All our personal experiences can become our greatest teachers for optimal growth. We evolve according to our reaction to each experience.

I knew that if I truly wanted to be happy, I would have to fall in love with myself. That meant no more self-sabotage, no more looking in the mirror and calling myself names, no more feeling horrible about overeating, or skipping a workout, or just plain making myself feel bad for living. So many of us focus on our outside relationships with significant others, family, and friends. We try to make sure they are happy and respect us or treat us kindly, but inside we are at war with ourselves. The real issue is the constant battlefield that lives in our heads. In order to reach self-love, we have to address the inner critic that tries to tear us down. I spent years blaming my childhood bullies for making me insecure. With a shrug of the shoulders I just accepted that this happened to me, as if to say, "Oh well, this is my story," but I was the biggest bully of all. My internal rage against myself was keeping me from everything I wanted. It had nothing to do with the bullies or outside influences but with how I was relating to myself. I could start being nice to me and stop thinking I couldn't love myself because of my shape or size. The fix: the Self-Love Experiment.

THE SELF-LOVE EXPERIMENT PROCESS

DURATION: THREE MONTHS

GOALS

1. Lighten up (emotionally, physically, spiritually, intellectually).

2. Increase self-confidence and be able to look in the mirror and say only kind things.

3. See myself the way my dog does (awesome, amazing, beautiful, quite possibly the coolest person in the world).

The Magic of Self-Care

THE MOST BASIC FORM of self-love is caring for yourself. We have to start with self-care. Let's get this right out of the way. Self-care is not about drinking your green juice or taking your vitamins every day and always keeping your diet super clean. It's not about incessantly working out or meditating. For some it may be, but that's because that is in alignment with that person. The most important thing is that you do what is in alignment with you. My paternal grandmother ate chocolate and drank coffee every day. For many years she drank alcohol quite frequently. And yet she was extremely healthy her entire life. She passed on at age ninety-four but never felt as though her choices hurt her. She was petite, fit, and happy. Have you ever noticed that there are certain people who seem to be able to eat or drink anything they want without the same result as others who put on weight or feel sluggish? It's because they don't pay attention to these things. The emotion around what we do is often more detrimental than what we actually do. What is important is how you *feel* about the things you do.

I used to think self-care meant being an A+ wellness warrior, which meant that each day I must ask myself, "Did I drink my green juice?" (check); "Did I do my workout?" (check); "Did I count my calories?" (check); etc. This way of life was exhausting, and I always felt like something was missing. I was trying so hard to control everything around me—my schedule, my body size, my habits, everything was neatly in a box—but my doctor diagnosed me with depression. I hated my job at the time, and I was silently suffering from drug addiction and body dysmorphia. Most of us have something we don't like about our appearance—a crooked nose, an uneven smile, or eyes that are too large or too small. And though we may fret about our imperfections, they don't interfere with our daily lives. But my insecurities were my obsession. I couldn't help but think about my flaws for hours each day. Before my Self-Love Experiment, I couldn't control my negative thoughts. My insecurities even interfered with my social life, as I started to avoid situations out of fear others would notice my flaws. This was an emotional disease that I was suffering from. The fix was finding self-love. But before I started my experiment, I used to be the master of "self-care." Sure, on the outside I was taking care of myself, by society's standards, but I hated myself and was depressed.

What kind of life is that?

As you can imagine, this wasn't real self-care. Because "caring" for yourself is loving yourself. I started to look at what self-care meant to me, and when I was honest I realized I didn't really like kale salad, I was sick of green juice, and I was burned out with yoga.

Self-care has nothing to do with what you do but with why you do it.

And the only reason we should do anything is because it makes us feel good. Because it brings us joy. I started to use joy as my barometer for self-care. If it brought me joy, I would allow it and enjoy it fully. If it felt forced, I wouldn't do it. This meant being okay with eating ice cream for breakfast (not every day, of course, but when I wanted it, I honored my desire) because I wanted to, without shame or guilt. But you know, the interesting thing is the more I loved myself, the less I craved sugar. Throughout my Self-Love Experiment my choices became naturally more healthful; they were never forced. The key is to be present with your joy in each moment, and let that be your guiding compass. For example, this meant canceling my yoga membership so I could have more time for hikes and nature walks. This meant booking a spontaneous trip to Paris to celebrate finishing my book and honoring my heart's calling to celebrate life. Self-care is our foundation; it is our intention and our daily focus. Naturally we want to be healthy, but healthy is not one-size-fits-all. What makes one person joyful and healthy is not the same for the next.

My mission was to address my self-care habits. I started with my appearance. Let's be honest. I had let myself go. By looking at my habits, I could see areas that needed attention in my life. I was wearing frumpy clothes and shoes that had holes in the soles. I went straight to my closet and took everything—I mean *everything*—out. My room was a giant pile of memories wrapped up in outfits I couldn't squeeze into anymore. For the past two years I had avoided mirrors as well as dressing rooms.

I rotated between pairs of stretchy pants; I hadn't worn jeans in eighteen months because I couldn't fit into my old size. I had a choice. I could keep avoiding the truth and pretend things were okay and stay stuck in being uncomfortable, or I could be a big girl, suck it up, and go buy the larger pants size, which meant admitting to myself that I was larger than I'd ever been before.

I looked at all my old clothes I couldn't wear and put them into piles:

1. Will never wear again, which became the donation pile.
2. Love so much, I can't part with nor can I fit into it; maybe wear again one day.
3. Currently wearing.

I realized there on that floor, glaring back at me, was a reflection of all my pain and self-shame. Eighty percent of my closet was a has-been. Old fabric I couldn't fit into, which only made me feel worse about gaining weight. As long as I had these piles in my closet, I wouldn't be able to let go of my past and accept where I was today. That meant donating everything that didn't bring me joy. If there were clothes in my closet I looked at and felt regret or sadness because I couldn't fit into them, they had to go. If there were clothes I loved so much because of sentimental value but couldn't fit into, I would use them for motivation. I couldn't move forward if my past was laughing at me every day.

After removing everything that no longer worked, I noticed the clothes were a reflection of my lack of upkeep on Shannon. Some of these items had holes in them, bras from five years earlier, which meant they clearly didn't fit. No wonder I felt so uncomfortable each day. I was squeezing my new-size body into the self of five years ago.

Restricting ourselves and forcing ourselves to fit into something that isn't meant to fit is a metaphor for our lives. By thinking there was something wrong with me because I had gained weight, I was avoiding the truth and not being real with myself. But in accepting my body, change could then take place.

I went to the store and upgraded my wardrobe. It felt like a miracle trying on clothes that actually fit. My body felt healthier, thinner, even pretty. "This is one small step in the right direction," I thought. I didn't realize that holding on to something as simple as clothes from five years prior was actually hurting my health and also preventing me from feeling good in my body. Squeezing all my curves into clothes three sizes too small was not a habit by choice. It was a habit of comfort. I was comfortable in my old size, and for years I was afraid to admit that I had gained weight. Lying to myself didn't hurt just my self-esteem—it also hurt my relationship with my body. Now that I was in clothes that felt good on my body, I walked with a little skip in my step. I held my head a little higher and I smiled more.

42

Self-care means learning how to treat ourselves with more respect.

It's possible we all lie to ourselves a little bit. Maybe we are afraid to admit something about ourselves that we are afraid to look at. We worry that if we address a situation then we will somehow be found out or exposed. But in this exact act of admitting what you are most afraid to admit, you will find clarity and truth. The process will help you become your own friend. It helped me, but I had to be willing to hold nothing back. I wanted to show up fully for me; it was time to be honest. How and where can you be more honest with yourself?

The word *self-love* feels funny for the majority of people. Self-love feels selfish. We are not trained to love ourselves. Because we are not used to it, it feels odd and uncomfortable for many of us. But we owe it to ourselves to care for ourselves. I discovered that the word *self-love* felt uncomfortable, so I focused on *self-care*. Self-care is somehow so much easier to approach than self-love—it feels less . . . huge. Instead of saying "I need to love myself," practice simply caring for yourself. A foundation for any healthy relationship is trust, and if we lie to ourselves, we don't have that. From there on out, I made a promise to always be honest with myself. In my own journey I had every interest in falling in love with myself, so acceptance was the order of the day, even in my plus-size body.

Ask yourself, "Which habit no longer serves me?" I looked at my daily habits and asked which habits no longer served me. I discovered that for many years my eating was on autopilot. By becoming more keenly aware of my overeating, I could then transform it. In order to do this, however, I also needed to remove the guilt. We all have habits, and many of them are ingrained into our routine. Often they help us function, but sometimes they hinder us. Ask yourself which habits are hindering your happiness, and be willing to take away the emotion from the habit and let the habit be in your life. As you take away the guilt and shame the habit will lessen, and if indeed it is time to let it go, it will be easy to release.

The reality is, when you're ready to make a change, it is easy. But you have to be ready. We all have certain habits that block us from being our best self. Many are unconscious or so ingrained in our daily routine that they often hurt our success at healing. Bad habits create more bad habits. But for the sake of our Self-Love Experiment, let's drop the idea of "good" and "bad." This pressure won't serve us.

Instead, let's look at every experience as an opportunity to learn and grow.

If you really want to change your life, you have to try something radically new. For me, it looked like being honest with myself. I wrote down on a piece of paper, "If you got yourself into this overweight body, you can get yourself out." What can you write on your own piece of paper? Maybe "I got into this debt; I can get myself

43

out." "I got into this troubled job; I can get myself out." Allow yourself to be very honest and own up to the fact that you are in this situation because you got yourself here. So guess what, beautiful? The fantastic news is, you can get yourself out. It's about accountability and acceptance.

But you also need the willingness to make a change. Before this moment I had a desire, which is different from being willing. You may desire a soul mate, but being willing to open your heart to new love is an entirely different story. You may desire to find your life purpose, but being willing to live without the comfort of a paycheck or a stale yet secure environment is a totally different notion. We must be willing, and in this willingness the change can truly take place.

I reflected on all of my previous behavior in trying to lose weight. It had always been such a struggle. I had felt so much pressure to drop pounds; meanwhile I would mentally beat myself up for not seeing a change. This self-hate fueled my weight gain. The radical change for me was a shift to accepting myself and relaxing in the journey. Instead of desperately needing to hit a goal, I treated everything as an experiment. This helped tremendously. Just like a scientist experimenting in a lab, there is no expectation about the outcome, because every trial that results in an error brings you one step closer to a breakthrough and a new discovery. Be like a scientist and be open to possibilities. Become the explorer of your own life adventure. I invite you to go on your own experiment, a journey into self-love.

When we are experimenting, the goal is not certain, and so we are able to revel in the joy of the experience. I had two choices: I could accept what I couldn't seem to change or I could work my butt off to change, even though working so hard was exhausting and proved to be unfulfilling. As the serenity prayer that is so central to twelve-step programs goes:

O God, give us the serenity to accept what cannot be changed,
the courage to change what can be changed,
and the wisdom to know the difference.

This became my guiding light. I had fought an uphill battle trying to lose weight, so my only other option was to accept my overweight body. In this acceptance, resistance was released, and the joy of the experiment could commence.

When you can allow yourself to be where you are instead of where you think you should be or even where you want to be, freedom prevails.

And in this freedom, self-acceptance and joy rush in. This is a much better place to make a change from. By accepting myself, I was able to invite love in. Instead of self-criticizing thoughts, I said kind things to myself, which made my weight-loss journey much easier, and I was more pleasant to be around. Have you ever noticed when things are flowing in your life and they seem easy? Maybe you got that job without much effort, you met the person of your dreams when you were least expecting it, or you earned a big bonus without thinking about it. A lot of the time things happen because of divine timing. When things happen naturally, it is because it is the right time. Sometimes we try to force things to happen before we are really ready. Trust in divine timing because when the timing is aligned, things will be easier.

The key to getting anything you want is patience, timing, and trust.

That's not to say don't keep trying, but it is important to honor the flow of life, and you specifically have a journey. And when you are truly ready, you will find the courage, the wisdom, and the motivation to make the changes necessary to see the results you truly desire. You picked up this book; something in you led you to these words and this message. So I know you are ready.

Think about a time in your life when things flowed and they felt very natural. Maybe you got into the school you wanted, you met your partner, or you found your dream home with little to no effort. These are all indications that you were ready. So if it feels like a struggle right now to make a change, recognize that it might not be the time. But there are certain things you can do to help yourself along. I wasn't ready before my experiment to make major life changes. Of course I didn't know it at the time, but I was comfortable in my stuckness and was still learning lessons I needed to learn in order to become more open to the process of the experiment. Not until I honored my heart's calling to go work overseas did things begin to click for me. I was already well into my experiment but wasn't seeing massive results. But by honoring my inner voice, which said, "Go, take your business and work from different countries around the world," things shifted for me. I began to make more healthful choices, I raised my standards, and I fell in love with life, which gave me more permission to be me, and I feel in love with me. If I were to ignore my inner voice and not act on the inspiration, I would not be expressing self-love.

The bottom line is: divine timing is everything, and change is easier when you're ready. But you need a focused plan to invite the

46

right opportunities to you. The second part is to accept what you can't change. At some point in your acceptance journey, you will rise up and say, "Enough. I am ready for real, lasting transformation." After you fully accept what you can't change, you may ask yourself, "Am I ready to change this? Is this habit ready to transform?" Most of the time your inner guide will say, "Yes, let's do this." You will feel motivated because—guess what? You are ready. Change is yours for the taking. Are you ready to make healthy change stick? I certainly was, and here is how I did it:

With self-compassion in my driver's seat I was equipped to dive even deeper into my self-care routine. The tool I used was the Me Matters list.

47

After only a couple of weeks into my Self-Love Experiment, I saw profound results. I had lost some weight, I felt more balanced, I had more opportunities coming my way, and I smiled a lot more. I wanted to keep the positive momentum going, so I created a Me Matters list. This is a list of the mandatory experiences that align with your soul's ideal day. I asked myself, "What does my ideal day look like? When do I feel like my best self?"

And I created a list to align to that vision. It looked like this:

* I exercise daily with joy and excitement.
* I enjoy my food and choose foods that make me feel alive and vibrant.
* I listen to my body and trust its guidance.
* I speak kindly to myself.
* I have daily cuddle sessions with my dog, Tucker.
* I go outside and play with the world.
* I remove food guilt and cherish my food fully.
* I add more adventure into my life with travel and exploration.

* I am location independent; I can work and play from anywhere in the world.
* I am compassionate and kind to others and myself.
* Instead of asking what I can get, I ask what I can give.
* I am grateful and turn all my expectations into appreciation.
* I meditate or do positive affirmations daily.

48

I printed out this list and mounted one on my vision board and carried the other one around with me in my purse. This became my guiding light forward. By having a daily Me Matters list I was able to stay focused and accountable. This helped me stay honest with myself as well. Ask yourself, "What does my ideal day look like?" I am not talking about the win-the-lottery, travel-the-world "ideal" day; I mean your practical, current lifestyle ideal day. How do you want to show up for yourself? What do you want to do daily to take care of you? That becomes your go-to list to show yourself that you matter.

The Me Matters list worked for me. Each day I made a promise to myself to show up more fully for me. This meant taking time to prioritize self-care. Each day, one moment at a time, I would check in with myself and ask myself what felt most joyful and healthy right at that moment. This led me to take midday power naps, workout more, and change my diet to more organic, healthful meals. Think about your own life and how your body has been trying to talk to you. It might have a message for you; what is it saying? Let your body be your friend as you move forward. But also define self-care for you. Self-care is personal; it is not an easy-to-follow routine that is the same for everyone; it is not cookie-cutter.

I once had a roommate who was extremely healthy by society's standards. She was obsessed with cooking her own meals and removing all pesticides from fruits and vegetables. As soon as she bought her food she would soak everything for exactly one hour and then cook everything in bottled, filtered water. She did yoga every day and meditated as often as she could. This seemed extremely healthy and to her it meant self-care. But she still got sick and often had digestive issues. On the other hand, at that time I wasn't eating healthful, organic foods; I was ingesting a lot of sugar and highly processed foods. We were opposites, but we could learn from each other. She taught me how to prepare foods in the healthiest manner possible, and I learned about organic foods from her, and I showed her that being strict one hundred percent of the time does not actually prevent you from being sick, because she actually got sick more than I did.

Self-care is an individual expression. It is not one-size-fits-all.

The goal is to feel healthy and happy, and you do this through self-care. No matter what your self-care routine looks like, the entry point is through the body. What we put in our bodies and on our bodies matters. Even the environment we live in matters. Self-care is a holistic, 360-degree approach to taking care of you.

Self-care can be about what you eat, what you wear, where you live, what you say, and what you think. It is all of you and how you relate to the world. Start showing up for you in new ways by being intentional about your self-care routine. Today my self-care routine is all about balance. I listen to my body—when it says it's full, when it says it's thirsty, when it says it's tired, I honor its needs. In turn, by listening to my body and making body care part of my routine, my skin has cleared up. I have more energy and I have even

49

lost a little more weight. It all comes back to love and taking loving action through self-care. And the reasons I was able to see results early on in my Self-Love Experiment is because I was letting love lead the way. I was taking clear action steps, such as working out more, traveling more, writing more, eating more organic food, all things on my Me Matters list, all these things that brought me joy. I did them all through the lens of self-love. Experiment with allowing self-love to guide you through your self-care practice; it certainly helped me.

50   While I was in my Self-Love Experiment I discovered something I was unaware of. I was settling. I was settling in a body I felt uncomfortable in. I was settling in an environment that wasn't comfortable. I was settling in my singlehood status, for I wanted a romantic partnership so badly, but I was scared of admitting that. I was settling in almost every area of my life. The more I took care of myself, the more it began to dawn on me: I had been settling. Through caring for myself more, I naturally raised my standards. The more attention I gave to myself, the more attention I realized I deserved. Saying this is not egotistical. This is about value. And I didn't value myself before. I was just going through the motions in life and trying to survive. I realized through my Self-Love Experiment that the added weight on my body, the choice to hide away from the world and remain single, was a protection mechanism. My ego was trying to protect me. I had at some point shut down emotionally and put up guards. My overeating and my lack of self-care before my experiment were a result of my giving up on love and, in some aspects, on my own life. I was afraid to look at the areas of my life that felt unfixable, unlovable, and unapproachable, and so I had been ignoring them. The Self-Love Experiment taught me how to breathe life back into the parts of me that I'd abandoned. I left a part of me in my childhood, the little me who never felt accepted or loved for who she really was, and I was stuck replaying

that same scenario and story as an adult. We do this from time to time. If we really want to reach self-love, we have to let go of that story and the wounded inner child still affecting our adulthood and learn how to bring ourselves back to life. We can do this by showing up for ourselves. One moment at a time, one step at a time. One choice at a time. Each day I took action to prioritize self-care. I went back to the wounded child inside and said, "I love you, dear little me. You are enough as you are." This small dedication to my healing transformed my entire experience of life. I raised my standards and started living more intentionally. Ask yourself, "What part of myself have I abandoned? What part of me needs love and care?" Visit your childhood wounded self and send little you some love. And today as you read this, start to think about ways you can prioritize your own self-care; your future self will thank you.

51

I DESERVE

my own love
and attention.

I CARE

and appreciate
all of me.

———

#MeMattersMantra

The Magic of Self-Compassion

*D*URING THE SELF-LOVE EXPERIMENT, I realized I had to get honest about the mental abuse I was bestowing on my body. My first step was to treat it kindly with words. Instead of emotionally abusing myself, I started to speak kindly to myself. Even though I was overweight and had stretch marks and cellulite, I could learn to love these "flaws" by being kind to them. My body was like a wounded, abandoned child, just trying to survive in the harsh world. I had mistreated it for so many years, punishing it for all my mistakes. But it wasn't my body's fault. My body was just a victim of a lack of love. It didn't know that its owner, me, didn't know how to love it. After all, I was doing the best I could. Isn't that all we ever do? We do the best we can, given our degree of self-understanding at the time. As Maya Angelou said, "Do the best you can until you know better. Then when you know better, do better."

I started by first changing the conversation I had with my body. Instead of blaming it, I would take bubble baths and rub my overweight belly and say, "I am so sorry for being so mean to you. I am sorry for abusing you, I love you, and I am glad you are part of me."

Day by day as I practiced kindness, along with physical action steps such as eating more healthful foods and drinking more water, my body began to change. The cellulite lessened, my waist showed more, I felt more connected to my best self, and I started to feel inner peace.

Talking nicely to myself was a good first step, but I recognized that I needed to physically nurture my body as well. I bought a lavender body cream, my favorite scent, and started a daily ritual of rubbing my body with the lotion while repeating positive affirmations:

54

"You're beautiful and perfect as you are."

"Your body is part of you and a reflection of love."

"I love you."

By treating my body with more daily love, my relationship with myself and others became healthier. I would no longer avoid mirrors or feel bad about my size. I stopped thinking everyone was judging me. Soon enough, I was actually proud of my reflection, as it reflected the love and care I was giving to myself.

Celebrating you is not egotistical; it is an act of self-love.

Think about a pet, child, or loved one. You often tell them you love them as you hug and squeeze them with joy. Why is it we can do this to others but not to ourselves? Give yourself the same love and attention you do to others, with confidence and pride. One way to build your inner self-love muscles is to listen to your body.

Part of my body-care routine was about learning how to listen to it. I used to punish my body and override its needs with sugar, binge eating, or self-deprecating thoughts. All that had to change, so instead of hating myself, I began to listen to myself. I woke up each morning and said, "What does my body want? What does it need?" It was clear my body wanted me to clean up my diet. So I started to experiment with different types of diets. I tried vegan, gained ten pounds, and was cranky *all* the time. I tried juice cleanses, and my skin cleared up, but I was always hangry (hungry plus *über* angry). I tried vegetarian, sugar-free, grain-free, soy-free, and none of them worked. But treating self-love as an experiment gave me an opportunity to try new things without shame, even if they didn't work out. That is what experiments are. We can release our attachment to the outcome, because with experiments, some things work while others don't. I adopted this principle to a new approach to life, which led me to a paleo-style diet of mostly protein from meat and tons of vegetables. My body responded instantly. I started to tone up again; I felt more mental clarity and I had more energy.

Paleo-style eating worked for me, but it is important to know one size does not fit all. For your Self-Love Experiment, try to explore different diets before you commit to one. If you have been feeling lethargic or run-down, or you get a lot of headaches or body aches, it could be your inner guide trying to tell you to look at your diet and make some changes. The amazing thing about this experiment is that I took my attention off the weight and the number on the scale, and by removing my focus on losing weight, the weight loss was able to happen naturally. My body healed.

Our bodies have abundant wisdom to share with us.

Our bodies can heal themselves if we get out of the way. I knew this on a fundamental level; now it was about trusting my body and letting it do its thing, without me interrupting. This meant not eating foods when I wasn't hungry. This meant listening to it when it said it needed rest, or when it nudged me for more movement. My body became my partner in healing, and I learned how to "love it and embrace it." I began to take longer walks with my dog, Tucker, and sleep more soundly. My body was leading me to health; I just had to get out of my own way. All of this led to more confidence and true self-acceptance.

During my experiment I made a conscious effort to refrain from negative self-talk and to practice kindness, and my body responded. Your mind is more powerful than you may realize. Think about what you've been saying about yourself and the situation you aspire to change. And then clean up those thoughts to a more compassionate dialogue.

Once you start prioritizing self-care, don't forget to be compassionate toward yourself.

Removing guilt and shame from anything you do is important, and you can do this by allowing yourself to be who you really are. I am a person who loves ice cream. Today I can eat it without guilt because I no longer deny myself things I love. There was a time when I couldn't have ice cream in the house because I would eat the entire container. I used to buy pints and eat half of one, then put dishwashing soap on the rest of it so I wouldn't eat it all, then I'd wash it down the drain. I did this as I flogged myself for eating ice cream in the first place. Today my relationship with food is

56

much more balanced. I can keep ice cream in the freezer because I love myself, and I now eat a bite or two then feel satisfied. I have strengthened all areas of my life by using self-compassion. What was once a turbulent relationship, mine with food, has transformed because I invited more love into the equation.

Self-love starts in the mind and how you talk to yourself about yourself.

You see, it is all love. We are either in the absence of what we want or in the presence of it. And when you allow yourself to have desires and you give in to them, this is an act of self-love. I am not talking about indulgence or gluttony, for that is not self-care. It is about being honest with and authentic to yourself. During my Self-Love Experiment, I learned to stop denying myself my truth, which is that I love food. I really, really love being able to eat and enjoy the flavors and textures of food and appreciate what a miracle food is. We get to experience eating, and eating is a form of love. I used to think eating was a horrible thing; I hated food because I thought it made me fat. I felt horrible for eating anything, especially foods I really wanted but felt I wasn't supposed to have, like ice cream and pizza, but once I dropped the story that food is bad and instead transformed it to food is love, my entire experience of life was renewed. I was able to keep ice cream and chips in my house and not binge on them; I was able to leave food on my plate; I stopped obsessing about food and started to focus more attention on life and living it more fully—all because I started with self-compassion. Which is being kind to you. So, my dear, can you let your guard down? Can you allow yourself to do the things you really want to do? That is the truest form of self-love. If you can't right at this moment, no worries; this book is dedicated to helping you become more compassionate to yourself so you can become your own best friend.

What does self-compassion look like? This looks like my new workout routine, a brisk nature walk without counting calories or wearing a Fitbit to keep track of how many miles, as I am being kind to myself while moving my body. Self-care and self-compassion are about removing guilt and shame from being you; it's about you honoring your true needs. It's about identifying your habits and behaviors and allowing yourself to be you. It is about allowing yourself to be who you really are, not who you think you should be or who society thinks you should be. Self-compassion at its core is about learning how to be gentle and kind to yourself in a world that pushes the opposite. Self-compassion is the foundation of self-love.

But most important, self-compassion is about allowing ourselves to be us, to eliminate the need to compare ourselves to anyone else. When we compare ourselves, we fall victim to our ego mind. We think mean thoughts about ourselves that we begin to believe are true. I learned that being kind to myself starts by stopping the comparison mentality. When I first started growing my business, I always compared myself to others. I looked at other authors and my own life coach and felt jealous because I wasn't as "far" along as they were. They had bestselling books and thousands of followers all celebrating their work. They were on TV sharing their message. I wanted that. But as long as I was comparing myself to them, I never felt good enough. I realized this pattern itself, of always looking outside myself for fulfillment, was keeping me from being fulfilled. Everything changed when I stopped looking at others and thinking I needed to be more like them and I started to show more of me. I have a saying I use with my entrepreneur clients: "The more you that you show, the more your business will grow." Which I found to be true: the more me I allowed to shine through, the faster my business grew. I stopped comparing myself to my mentors and other authors and just celebrated me. You can apply this saying to any area of your life: "The more me I show, the more my dreams will grow!" "The more me I show, the more my relationships will flow." "The more me I show, the easier my life will flow." Try it out—this is a powerful mantra you can use in your own life to overcome insecurities and setbacks.

The Self-Love Experiment is an experiment, which means some things will work for you, while others may not. It's important to exercise compassion along your journey and let go of the drive for perfection. I made sure to be kind to myself and treat the entire process as an experiment.

Until we learn self-compassion, we can't fully love ourselves.

When we don't love ourselves, we feel disconnected from our source—the loving energy within—and it is difficult to connect with our best self and those around us. Most of us are taught to be compassionate to others, but we never learn how to be kind or compassionate with ourselves. During my Self-Love Experiment, I decided to exercise compassion by being kinder to myself. I made it a point to check in daily and celebrate the good things I was doing and how far I had come. I became my own cheerleader. This was difficult at first, and if you haven't practiced being kind to yourself, it may be hard for you, too. You can do this by asking yourself, "What am I learning?"

Identifying the life lessons you are learning is a powerful way to exercise compassion. Instead of focusing on how far you still need to go, shift your attention to how far you've come. I encourage you to try it out for yourself. Write your own "what am I learning?" letter. What have you learned so far?

60

The more me
I show, the more
MY LIFE WILL
FLOW.

#MeMattersMantra

The Magic of Self-Trust

*O*NCE I REALLY PRACTICED self-care and being compassionate with myself, I started to trust myself more. Lack of self-trust is at the core of why most of us feel unhappy. Many of us don't trust ourselves, and we don't trust life, but when you practice self-care and you are kind to yourself, self-trust becomes natural. Trusting yourself is about believing in yourself and knowing that you matter. Your dreams and desires are part of trusting yourself. As I explored more of my Self-Love Experiment, and the more I started to show up for myself and practice self-care, the more my dreams begged to be realized.

The more I loved myself, the easier it was to say yes to my dreams.

While writing this book, a major dream of mine was recognized and actualized. I wanted to live and work overseas for six months. I had left corporate America several years before in the hopes of being able to work from anywhere in the world, but I wasn't really doing that. I had fallen into a routine, and I felt numb and bored with my life. I wanted a location-independent business, one that would allow me to work and play from anywhere in the world, but at the time I was working from my own home office and stuck in a routine. The Self-Love Experiment gave me permission to dream again, and through self-trust I was reminded of the power of our dreams, that we can live a life that makes us happy. Trusting yourself is saying, "I matter."

Something unexpected happened during my Self-Love Experiment. Once I reached self-love, surprisingly I still had feelings of worry. I wondered, "How long is this going to last? I don't want people to be jealous or think I am showing off." I realized this was just my ego, my fear-based voice trying to sabotage my success. Our egos will always try to bring us down, especially when we are making headway. We have a choice: we can listen to this inner critic, or we can choose the loving voice. For me, I leaned into love. My loving voice stepped in and reminded me that I have done tremendous work on myself and that this was the reward of true healing and growth. And I can't control other people's worries or perceptions of me, but we do owe it to ourselves to be happy and live our dreams daily. Self-trust is about letting go of outside pressure and letting yourself shine.

The bottom line is that you deserve so much happiness, and allowing yourself to feel it is the ultimate form of self-love. When you feel happy and joyful, hug yourself and say, "Welcome to the goodness—all of my hard work has paid off."

Let yourself bask in the beauty of you.

At the start of my experiment, I couldn't help but wonder how important our environment is to feeling self-love. Not just our physical environment, but also our home and the body we live in. I didn't feel good in my environment, so I moved. As I mentioned, a big dream of mine was to live and work overseas for an extended period of time. But in order to follow through on this dream, I needed to trust myself and trust this dream. Living our dreams requires courage, and we get courage by taking action. The more we trust ourselves, the easier it is to take action. I trusted my dream and myself, and during the six months that I lived and worked from overseas, I felt a deep connection to myself. This helped me build up my inner trust muscles even more. I became more self-aware and really tuned in to my body's needs and desires. I took much better care of myself not only because I changed my environment but also because I had trusted myself. You see, when we follow through on the inspiration that comes to us, when we take action on our desires, we send a message to ourselves that it is okay to listen to our own hearts. We create a powerful relationship with our own inner guides. Your inner guide is your friend and is trying to nudge you into directions that will bring you more joy. When you trust this guidance, you will see your life open up into more possibilities and joy.

In order to thrive we have to feel safe and trust our environment and ourselves. I learned the power of physical space and how important where we live is to feeling joy. Does your environment lift you up and inspire you? I believe it is a critical part of our self-love expression. *A Course in Miracles*[5] says our outside world is a reflection of our internal state. This means that what you think on the inside will manifest on the outside. Cleaning out my closet was a good first step, but I had to look at all areas of my environment: my kitchen, my office, and my transportation. My Jeep was my dream car and a gift I'd bought myself to celebrate leaving my corporate job, but it was messy. Dog hair and old juice bottles and magazines were scattered in the back seat. One day it dawned on me that the stalls I felt in my life could be because of the clutter in my physical world. My transportation at the time was a reflection of my internal body. I had carb-loaded with fat and sugar for years, and my inside was yearning for healthful, clean eating. Once I realized the connection, I immediately cleaned out my car. Within days I lost a few pounds, I got three new coaching clients, and one of my articles was picked up by *Entrepreneur* magazine, an outlet I had spent nine months pitching. These aren't random coincidences; they are all connected. I cleaned up my energy by cleaning my physical space and transportation, which affected my life as I attracted more opportunity into my life. Look at your physical environment. Does it feel expansive and joyful, or is it messy and cluttered? Part of the Self-Love Experiment is to make sure your environment reflects a loving, kind atmosphere. Remove any negative things that no longer serve you, such as old pictures or items from your past that you no longer need, and invite in new energy with things that bring you joy. I encourage you to clean out your car or whatever physical space you use for transportation. This energetically sends a message that you want a smooth ride in life, and the universe responds. If we buy things that are loving and joyful, we extend our energy into these things. When we buy something that doesn't bring us joy, we continue the pattern of self-shame and regret. Do yourself a favor and spend money only when you are in a joyful state. This will help you invest in items that make you happy, and it will make your home more inviting for you.

My environment, the physical place where I lived, was soon a reflection of peace and joy. I decorated my home base in Portland, Oregon, with quality things from my travels. I cleaned up my environment by upgrading my home as well with small, simple things like indoor air plants and succulents. All of these seemingly small

65

steps were inspired by my inner guide. I trusted myself to listen to the inspiration that came to me. All our inspiration, the gut feelings, and the desires that pop into our head are part of our life plan. We are receiving guidance all the time, guidance from our higher self, and this guidance gives us insight into what will bring us true joy and happiness. Our job is to trust this guidance and listen to it. The more we listen to it, the stronger our inner faith and trust muscles become. In trusting my inner voice, through my Self-Love Experiment, I was urged to raise my standards. When you listen to your inner voice, you may be invited to raise your standards, too.

When you love yourself, it is easier to make your dreams come true.

WHEN I LOVE MYSELF

it's easier to see imbalances in my life.

#MeMattersMantra

The Magic of Self-Acceptance

THE NEXT PHASE IS self-acceptance. This feels like peace. Self-acceptance is where you allow yourself to be who you are. Instead of running, changing, or trying to fix, you surrender to what is.

Self-acceptance is joy.

My grandma, my mother's mom, Rosemarie Rusnak, was always overweight. About a hundred and fifty pounds overweight most of her life; I always considered her my big grandma. As a child I never judged her or thought there was anything wrong with her. I just loved her. As I grew into an adult and started putting on more weight, I asked her one day if, after living an entire lifetime in an overweight body, she had any advice, any wisdom, she could share. She was very clear with me:

Don't waste time with negative thoughts.

Life is too short to spend flogging yourself or feeling bad about any part of yourself. She said that a bright side of her being over-weight was how people enjoyed her company—she knew that her friends and family felt that her soft and fluffy hugs were some of the best hugs to be had in the world. She told me that she felt that society and culture put a lot of pressure on people to change, even though when it comes to the relationship between body weight and health, scientific studies will say one thing, then a couple of months or years later they change perspective. Being overweight is not an issue unless you make it an issue. Of course we want to be healthy and make smart choices, but that first has to start in the mind. Being kind and compassionate to yourself is key. She told me:

Loving yourself has nothing to do with how you look or your size. It is about how you live.

My grandmother's words will always stay with me. She taught me that because self-acceptance is not what you do or don't do, it is about allowing yourself to be you in your own life. Let yourself be you. Accept yourself as you are, because you are magnificent.

There are many layers to self-love, and approaching it from just the outside and how you look will never give you the results you desire. For me, I had to also look at where and how I was spending my time. Most of my evenings were about watching Netflix shows and scrolling Facebook. Not productive at all. My fix: through the Self-Love Experiment I made a list of all the things I wanted to do and learn. So I made a reading list of books I wanted to read and topics I wanted to write for new articles. Instead of mindlessly eat-ing in front of the TV, watching boring reruns, I drank tea in my new lovely mugs from India and took online courses and read new books. This filled my soul with excitement and kept me energized.

I had always valued learning, but my Self-Love Experiment led to my actually seeking out new education opportunities and seminars. I had always wanted to take a Doreen Virtue course; in this process I signed up for an Angel Card Reading class and became a Certified Angel Card Reader. I also worked with my mentor and friend, Gabrielle Bernstein, and took her digital Spirit Junkie Masterclass, which earned me another credential. I discovered Reiki, an energetic healing practice; my inner guide was leading me to new methods of healing and mind-growing courses. I started taking language classes, which were divine. The more I showed up for my desires, the things I'd always wanted to learn, the more I liked myself. The more accepted I felt. My Self-Love Experiment allowed me to show up more fully for myself and invest in mind-expanding programs, which led to new opportunities for my business and me.

> Our time is the most important form of currency we have. When you cherish yourself, you spend your time wisely.

In my coaching and live workshops, people often ask, "How do I find time to do what I love when I am so exhausted at the end of the day?" Maybe you can relate. Many people don't love what they do, which actually pulls more energy and time because it is draining on the mind and body. The short answer is: we will find time and energy for what is most important to us. (This idea originates from the Pursuit of Excellence, a personal development seminar series on this topic.) If we are burned out from what isn't working, we will not have energy to do what we want. So instead focus your attention on what you want first and watch how your energy shifts.

I worked with a client who felt this way. She didn't like her day job; she wanted to be a writer, but at the end of the day she was spent. I encouraged her to write first thing in the morning for seven days, and this small shift changed everything for her. Because she carved out a special time each day to do what brought her joy, she started to feel more joy in other areas of her life. The next week when we talked she had written an entire chapter (one she had started and worked on previously for months). She had more energy throughout the day, and she came home to write as well. She continued this practice and found a literary agent to represent her book. It was nothing short of a miracle, which happened because she put her passion first.

71

Working hard for something we don't care about is stress. Working hard for something we love is called passion.[6]
—SIMON SINEK

What passion have you been putting on the back burner? Put that passion first and watch how you have more energy and time available to you. Remember, the Self-Love Experiment is an experiment—the results are less important than the journey. The Self-Love Experiment can help you get back on track with your own goals. Because the bottom line is: when we show up for ourselves, we show up for the world. And the more you show up, the more you feel seen and appreciated. Essentially it all comes back to self-acceptance, as this is a strong foundation for self-love.

As I started to show up more fully for myself, I noticed a contradiction between my habits and my outcomes. Previously, so much of my attention was on losing weight. I wanted so much to lose weight, I felt my happiness and self-love were tied to my being a certain number on the scale, but as I dove into my experience, *pleasure* became my primary focus. Pleasure in art, writing more, quality food, nature, travel, enriching conversations—the experience of really embracing life became a priority. I stopped denying myself pleasure. One thing I often ask my coaching clients is, "When do you feel like your best self?" I realized I had never really asked myself that, and when I did, I was excited to learn that it is when I am traveling and writing and in nature and eating wonderful food. So you can see my previous behavior of denying myself things that I loved, like food or adventurous trips, was directly in conflict with being true to myself. As I started to reprioritize my life, pleasure became my North Star. I committed to myself and did activities that brought me joy. What would this look like for you? What if you committed to a life of more pleasure? For me, this looked like attending more cultural events and art shows, taking more trips, and writing more for fun, just for me, instead of trying to meet a deadline or write for some specific outcome. Joy was found in the mini-moments, the pleasure-seeking efforts, which brought me into more self-awareness, allowing me to accept myself more fully. Self-love is layered, but when we approach it as an experiment, it becomes more of an adventure and a true joy in life. We can approach pleasure with more passion.

I invite you to think about what brings you pleasure. Is it wonderful food? Then maybe cook yourself a meal from a new cookbook. Do you enjoy being creative? Then maybe pull out your paints and start to create more art or sign up for an art class. Maybe you have a vision board, with loads of travel photos. Then start researching your next trip and actually put down a deposit toward that goal. Pleasure is a key part of love. Just like a romantic relationship, pleasure is part of falling in love. If you allow yourself to be in the process of pleasure, then you can enjoy your passion guilt free. The more pleasure you seek, the more joy you feel, and in this joy you will feel accepted. You will see that you matter. A shift for me was in my experience of life. One of the ways I reached self-love was by honoring my natural tendencies and trusting the inspiration I felt from my heart. There were days when I would feel pressure to go to the gym or eat a salad, when really I wanted to relax and unwind with some popcorn or potato chips. There is a popular meme going around Facebook that reads, "Some days you eat salads and go to the gym. Some days you eat cupcakes and refuse to put on pants. It's called balance." The key is to recognize that balance is part of a well-lived life. I stopped feeling guilty for eating cupcakes or certain foods that society says are bad. I began to look at my natural urges, and I gave into them. I would buy a gourmet cupcake and eat two or three bites and then feel satisfied. Before, I would have gobbled it all up with shame. Once I removed the guilt and shame tied to eating, I naturally craved less. You may notice that the more in tune you become with your own desires, the less guilt you will feel. Because you will see they are signatures to your life fulfillment. The more you trust yourself, the easier it is to accept yourself. When we can honor our natural tendencies, we allow ourselves to be who we really are. We honor our truth. And in honoring our true self, we show up more fully.

73

I APPRECIATE ALL THAT I AM AND WHO I AM BECOMING.

#MeMattersMantra

me, as I am in each moment. Leaning into love is about discovering the power of you.

Ask yourself if you've been holding back and not allowing yourself to be you. During my experiment, I sat down and did something I had never thought to do before: I thanked my body. I wrote a compassionate letter to the one part of me I had hated for so many years. This radically deepened my love for myself and helped me feel happier in my own skin. My letter went like this:

Dear Body,

153

I can't believe I've never said this before. My dear body, it's long overdue, but you need to hear this from me. You need to know that you are magnificent. You need to know that I love you.

You are incredibly beautiful. All of you—every expanded stretch of skin, every inch is a miracle. I finally see you for what you are. A beautiful manifestation of my profound humanness. You are part of me, and finally I can see the truth: you are not the enemy. You never were.

For years I would pinch you, cry out into the dark night, praying for a thinner body, a different frame, a smaller stomach. I hated myself because I despised you. I prayed for you to be different, thought my life would be better when you were "not you" but smaller, thinner, not so chubby, not thick or round. I wanted you to change. I needed you to change in order for me to have a confidence in myself. But the miracle came not in you changing but in the change in my heart. For the first time in my thirty-five years of life, I finally see you for you. The glorious aspect of being human that you are.

You, dear body, are a gift to this world. Why? Because there is no other body in this entire world exactly like you. You are one of a kind, and I celebrate you for all that you have endured.

It was much easier to focus on what was wrong with you than on what was wrong in my life: the relationships that weren't fulfilling, the job that sucked my soul, the low bank account, and the unmet expectations. I could avoid it all as long as I focused on my disdain for you. You made it easy to run from what I need most: self-love.

It was never you. You, my dear body, are a glorious part of me. In all that you do, you help me be me. Without you I wouldn't be here. For decades I thought it was your fault— even still, you stayed by my side. You helped me dream bigger, reach for more, and play with the world in new ways never before explored.

You are my protector. My house. My temple. You have allowed me to do things I could have never achieved without you. I am thankful for you. You, dear body, hold my heart, the one that told me to listen to its intuitive guidance and leave my depression and corporate career behind so I could discover my passion as a writer. You held my heart, the one that cast a net out to reach for bigger dreams. You, dear body, have the hands to help me type my thoughts out into form.

You, my dear body, hold my brain, the one that overthinks and analyzes life in a way that gives me a deeply filled passion for what is possible. You, dear body, have stood by my side, daily embracing me for me. It's time for me to accept you for you as you are. Not when you lose more weight, not when you meet your soul mate, not when you get the new book deal— now, body, I accept and love you right now.

Today, I am thankful for you. For without you I wouldn't be me. The years of hate helped me find love. You helped me become more compassionate, more loving, more

APPRECIATE HOW YOU LOOK

APPRECIATE HOW YOU LOOK

understanding, and more patient. You, dear body, have taught me how to be me in a world that wants me to be different from what I am; you have given me the courage to be authentically me.

I promise to love you as you are in each moment of our life. I will speak kindly to you and practice compassion. I will treat you with respect and trust your guidance. I promise to be your friend and love you the way you are.

Dear body, I am thankful for you. Because out of our struggles I have found my strength, I've found a true friend, and together we can do so much more. I'm on your side now. I choose to accept you and love you for all that you have been, all that you are, and all that you are becoming.

155

Thank you for being you, all of you, as you are, because stretch marks, extra padding, chubby cheeks, and all, I embrace you, because without you, we wouldn't be here. I love you, dear body. You are me and part of my experience of life.

Thank you.

Love, Me

I kept this letter close to my heart and reread it often when I needed encouragement and more compassion.

Can you write a letter to your deepest pain point? Take your own Self-Love Experiment to the next level by writing a personal, heartfelt letter to your insecurity and pain. Write to the thing you hate most about you, what it is you want to heal. Send this aspect of you more love through a compassionate letter to yourself.

I AM *an expression of love.* I ALLOW *myself to shine my* GORGEOUS *light.*

#MeMattersMantra

Appreciate What You Have to Offer

PERFECTIONISM IS A SILENT killer. It robs us of joy, possibilities, and seeing things clearly. In my pursuit of "perfect" I've tried to change myself; I spent years in a skinny body, as well as decades in a chubby one. I suffered through eating disorders, all in a vain effort to fit in and be accepted. To be seen for who I feel I am.

I know you might be waiting for the big reveal. As you participate in the Self-Love Experiment, you might be waiting for the results. You might want me to tell you I lost all the weight, I found my soul mate, but I am still overweight and single. Maybe you are looking for the outcome of my Self-Love Experiment, the big "I lost all the weight, I am thin, lean, and happy." Well, that's not this story. I am happy, yes, extraordinarily so, but my happiness is not dependent on my body, or my size or shape, or my relationship status. It has nothing to do with the scale. Today I feel beautiful, and that is the magic of the Self-Love Experiment: I am no longer waiting to be someone else. It hasn't always been this way. There were days when the shame and guilt took hold. The pressure to be something I was not was enormous. The self-blame took over and affected my actions.

Before my experiment, the thing is, no matter how much self-love I tried to feel, I actually started to believe that I was broken because I was chubby. I allowed the world to tell me who I was. That is, of course, until I discovered real self-love. When I made it my full-time mission to eradicate these false beliefs and truly fall in love with my body, I no longer felt shame for being me.

We can spend our whole lives looking for answers outside of ourselves, or we can turn inward and feel what actually feels right in our heart.

But society, family, and our cultures still put pressure on us. In my experiment, I dug deeper, then it clicked. I thought, What if we have it all wrong?

What if the body we live in, no matter its size, is a gift?

What if the way people treat us is a reflection of them, not us?

What if shame and judgment are just a stand-in for a lack of love?

What if my body isn't something that needs to be fixed, but the only real thing needing healing is the belief system that something was wrong with me?

Every time I visit my doctor, we high-five in celebration of my status. I'm as fit as a fiddle and a healthy woman, he says. Yes, I'm overweight, but that doesn't mean I'm unhealthy or flawed on the inside.

No one can make you feel inferior without your consent.

When we stop letting our insecurities win, when we stop giving them power, when we stop negotiating with ourselves, we can see the truth.

I hope that anyone suffering from feelings of inferiority seeks self-approval. Love yourself, and you'll be free. Chances are you have something about you that you want to change. Instead of running from that thing, embrace it, love it, show it to the world. When you reveal your authentic self, the world will reveal back.

> When you value yourself and show up for you, the world will show up, too.

If you are negotiating with your insecurities, this means you are letting them get the best of you.

> The more attention we put on unwanted things, the easier it is for unwanted things to take over.

Here are eleven truths I learned when I stopped negotiating with my insecurities:

1. People will accept you only *when you accept yourself.*
2. What others say and do is a reflection of them, not of you.
3. No one can make you feel "less than" without your permission.
4. We see only what we want to see, when we are ready to see it.

5. Happiness comes from the inside, not from the outside.
6. The size of your body does not make you less of a person.
7. You are as beautiful as you allow yourself to feel.
8. The size of your body does not determine what you are capable of. Your heart and mind do.
9. You can never judge a person's insides by their outsides.
10. You're bigger than your body.
11. How you feel is more important than how you look.

Martha Beck wrote an article for *O, The Oprah Magazine* in March 2016 called "Hurt So Good." In the feature she explains that our bad habits, our deep-seated issues, and damaging behaviors actually do a lot more for us than we give them credit for.

For example, someone who can't stop binge eating and someone who seems to attract drama around every turn may not have a lot in common on the surface, but upon a deeper look, they each have what psychologists call secondary gains. A secondary gain is an attachment to the gain received from the habit, addiction, or self-sabotaging situation.

Ask yourself what problem you've been trying to get rid of but can't.

Now ask yourself what advantages you get from having this problem.

To free yourself you need to find a new pattern. In my life-coaching practice, I work with clients to identify their secondary gains. What is it you get by having these habits? Most of the time they look at me as though I've lost my mind. After all, we do therapy and read personal development books and hire life coaches to try to heal our pain, not look at what it gives us. But upon deeper inspection, we see that the situations reveal a deep need that is unmet—every single time. For example, I was working with a client who was always frantic and busy. She was a life coach and had a YouTube channel that supported her mission. In our session she expressed, "I don't know how to relax, I can't stop, I feel like I have to be creating and making new videos." I asked what her life would look like if she didn't fill up all her time with "busyness." What would it look like if she did relax or did play more? At first she said that would be amazing—"I don't know how to do it, but that's what I want." Then we dove deeper, and she realized that living a life with downtime felt like a setback to her; if she wasn't creating or making new videos, then maybe she thought she would become irrelevant or left behind in the hustle of it all. Her secondary gain from her busyness was that her busyness kept her preoccupied. If she wasn't busy creating new videos or trying to write more blog content, she would have to look at the areas of her business that weren't working. She didn't have many paying clients and hardly had any money coming in. She masked this lack by working harder so she wouldn't have to address the core issue: fear, that she felt undeserving of receiving money for her talent and knowledge.

You see, what's happening is not that she doesn't know how to slow down or relax. Her hustle attitude is a built-in protection mechanism, as most of our addictions, habits, and problems are, because many of us get our needs met through suffering.

We can learn through either passion or pain.

We feel as though our problems are hurting us, but they are in our lives because we gain something from them. Through my own research and life experience I discovered that our secondary gains, although they hurt so bad, actually make us feel good, if even in the moment they provide temporary relief from what it is we are unwilling, or not ready, to face. My overeating for years was my attempt to mask my truth feelings of wanting romantic love. If I didn't overeat, I would have to face the fact that I was lonely and really wanted romance. Ask yourself what your current habits and problems are giving you—this is the secondary gain.

It comes down to three main categories: freedom, fulfillment, or acceptance.

Identifying these categories and seeing what you get from each can help you break the habit. When you feel free, fulfilled, or accepted, your needs are met. These are your core desires and what your secondary gains are trying to give you.

Inspiried by Martha Beck, the fix to our habits, addictions, and problems is to designate some Me Matters time. I call it the Me Matters session. This is ten to fifteen minutes of uninterrupted time dedicated to giving yourself what you need most. If you crave freedom but feel trapped at your job, schedule a fifteen-minute walk outside of the office. This will give you more clarity and freedom. If you want more fulfillment, instead of spending your tax refund on new clothes you know you won't wear, look at putting money into savings for that trip overseas you've been dreaming about. If you want acceptance, stop being there for everyone and overextending yourself, and be kind to you. These are Me Matters sessions; schedule them throughout your day. I wanted acceptance; this was a big need of mine, and I turned to food to feel comforted and loved. Once I identified this, I started to think about other ways I could get my needs met. When I wanted acceptance, I dropped everything to do an extra-long cuddle session with my furry fella, Tucker. This was a powerful exercise that helped me heal my overeating patterns.

As Martha Beck says, by freeing up time to treat yourself with compassionate attention, problems you thought would never, ever go away will begin to weaken. And some will disappear entirely.

You will gain a direct route to what you once accessed through dysfunctional suffering and will find the peaceful, gentle, powerful rhythm of your own right life.

Ask yourself the same thing. What reward do you think you get from your most frustrating problem? What Me Matters session can you schedule?

As you start to identify your secondary gains and you work on releasing them, it is important you stay focused on your goal. Most of us look to results to show us we are on track and doing the right thing. When we see results, we stay motivated and we keep going. If we don't see results, we usually give up, abandon our dream early, or, at the very least, become frustrated and angry. But the path to self-love is not straight. We may not see results right away, which is why it is super important to focus on the reasons why we want what we want. Fitness coaches and trainers say it takes at least three to four weeks to see real results from a regular fitness routine. That's almost thirty days of creating a new habit, so:

The key to getting what you want is consistency, patience, timing, and trust.

The more consistent you are, the easier it is to form strong habits that are built on a solid foundation. Instead of looking for results to keep you on track, focus on your reasons why you started. When you *show up consistently* for yourself, you will start to see results. This is a beautiful process that will help you stay on track.

Self-love is about showing up for you and your dreams. This means that the reasons you start something are way more important than the results you see.

I call this approach to life "reason over results." Focus on your reasons for doing something instead of on the results. A powerful example of this concept is me writing this book. All of my insecurities and honest reflections came up with each new sentence I typed. I worried no one would read it. People would write bad reviews, and my publisher would deem me a horrible author and I'd be blacklisted from the industry. All these fears popped up daily during the entire process of writing this book. For months I felt this uncomfortable pain resting deep in my stomach. Yet I continued to forge forward. I could have easily looked for results to keep me going. A book advance, which I didn't have while writing the book, losing weight, or men asking me out for dates—none of it was there or happened as fast as I wanted. I was writing purely because it was in my heart to share; that was my reason. I was looking for love and focusing on my health daily despite the results the world was reflecting. Sometimes it takes a little while for the universe to catch up with your new desires.

Don't get distracted by what is. Focus on what might be; focus on what you want.

Instead I focused on my why, because I had to. If I didn't write this book, I would not be honoring my true path. I would be leaving a stone unturned. The results of this book, the outcome of writing this, are completely out of my control, but my reason for writing is that I had to. I needed to. My *Why?* is *Why not?* I have no control over the outcome, but I could be present in the process.

As I kept writing, day after day, word after word, the book slowly came together. As I wrote what I was living and sharing, I discovered real self-love. I trusted the process. There were moments when I stared at my screen, wondering why the words were so hard to get out; there were other days I thought how good, this book is so good, then moments later I'd think it was horrible. I felt like the entire book and message was crap. Why? Because I am human—and that is what fear does. It comes in and tries to convince us to stop. When we act on inspiration, when we push forward without seeing real results, the ego will do everything in its power to try to get you to quit. This is when you roll up your sleeves and pull out your motivation by returning to your why. Why did you start?

We do things not for the results but for the experience.

We think we want results, but our soul craves the experience. So I surrendered fully to the book-writing process—to the Self-Love Experiment that I had committed myself to. I let go of all expectations, and then the words flowed. They came out smoothly and with great ease. I felt grace step in and bring energy into my project, all because I let go of the outcome and instead focused on the process.

One of my author friends said she is writing her next book because she wants it to be a *New York Times* bestseller. I have another friend who said she wants to be a TEDx speaker so she can get more clients and be better known. When I hear things like this, I always worry, because my friends are doing what I, like so many of us, used to do: put expectations on our dreams. When we do something in order to get something else, we have already lost sight of the purpose.

The experience is the reward; the outcome is not as important. The real learning and growth happen in creating, working, and doing the process of the goal. Don't skip over the magnificent aspects of the process. Notice today if you are more focused on the results you want to see versus the reason you started. If so, you may be feeling frustrated because you aren't seeing the result you'd hoped. Before you give up on your goal and abandon yourself, show up fully by returning to your reasons why. This book wouldn't be in your hands if I were focused on results. I wrote the entire book before I had a book advance because I believe in myself and this message, and I dedicated myself to the process. Part of really reaching self-love is dedicating yourself to the process. The process of what you love, the process of self-care, and even the process of the journey. The journey is the reward, as the Chinese proverb says. One moment at a time, step by step, I could let my why drive me forward. Your reasons why are more important than the results. Let your why drive you. Ask yourself what your why is. What are your reasons for wanting what you want?

Once we start dedicating ourselves to approaching and caring for ourselves, we may see a shift in those around us. When I first left my corporate job, I was living with a man who wanted things to stay the same. I became a travel writer while we were together, and I started to write for local newspapers and get clear about my new life and what I wanted for myself. Which meant I was taking more trips, away from the comfort of our old regular routine. What was happening was I was practicing self-love and being more true to me. I was choosing self-love and showing up for me. This put a strain on our relationship big-time. He wanted things to be the same, but I was no longer the same person. I had outgrown my old self. What I share with coaching clients and in my own life is the concept of "bounced out."

Bouncing out is when your energy no longer aligns with that of

the people or situations around you. You vibrate yourself out because your desires and needs have shifted. My bounce out looked
like I had left my corporate job and now craved freedom. I loved
this person very much, but our points of view and choices were
now conflicting. It caused many fights and even more sleepless
nights. I felt so conflicted because I was growing as a person and
becoming more spiritually awake, and I wanted a partner who
could come along with me. But I quickly learned:

Not everyone is supposed to come along with us when we change.

I fought for months to try to hold on to the relationship and
force myself to fit in the box we had created together. But my wings
were restless. I needed to fly.

I finally got up enough courage to leave the relationship; it was
one of the toughest things I ever did because I wanted us to work.
I wanted that person to be my one. But as I grew into my self-love
practice, I grew away from some people, including people I once
loved. I loved him, but I loved myself more, and I needed to honor
the direction my life was heading. And I knew the best thing I could
do for my future self was to let that relationship go.

We can't hold on to things that are meant to be let go of.

Eventually the tipping point came when my desire to change
and honor my new direction in life was stronger than my desire to

stay the same. We all will get to this space, where we are confronted head-on with our past conflicting with our future. We have bounced out of what once felt right. It doesn't mean we made a mistake or we are off track. Staying in the situation is what causes stress in our life. Your inner guide is guiding you, and trusting that inner voice, even in the face of fear, will help you move into your ideal life faster. I was terrified to let go of what I'd worked so hard to maintain, but my inner voice became so loud I couldn't ignore it anymore. Staying in the situation that I had bounced out of energetically would have been settling. We must honor our own phases of our life. Bouncing out is quite often not a bad thing. Your soul is growing, so bouncing out just means that you've outgrown what you once needed to grow into.

Our old self will often grasp desperately, trying to hold on, but our new self eventually shines through. We must keep honoring the nudge and inner conviction that we matter and trust the newness that is emerging. Remember: our desires are important.

Everything always works out the way it should.

Recognize that you will bounce out of situations, though your fear will want you to stay. What it boils down to is:

Your desire to change must be greater than your desire to stay the same.

168

Your desire to change and trust the change will be for your greatest good and will lead you forward. My dear, give yourself more credit; if you feel like you've outgrown something in your life, you've bounced out, and that is a good thing. It means that you have grown into the person you wanted to become. So allow the rhythms of your life to unfold gracefully. Bouncing out is a blessing. Ask yourself: Is there a situation you feel you have energetically bounced out of but are afraid to let go of?

I EMBRACE
all that I am,
and I'M PROUD
of how far
I'VE COME.

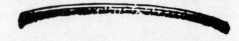

Appreciate the Unknown and the Space in Between

*I*N YOGA CLASS ONE DAY on the mat, the instructor was talking about a situation where one of her friends said, "Not everyone is interested in pursuing their full potential." She explained how this caught her off guard. As a yoga instructor, she prides herself on endurance and the pursuit of potential. The class theme became potential and inviting in our better self to be present in the moment. Because we are one with our future self, there is no separation when you are truly in the art of becoming. Which is the place I arrived at in my self-love journey. I no longer was desperate to reach some far-off goal. I was actually more excited about the becoming, the journey, and the moment that matters in this space, the potential of now. As you go through your own Self-Love Experiment, remember that now is more important than tomorrow. And now is more critical than yesterday. The only way you can truly affect tomorrow and reach your goals is to address them today with your habits. What are you doing today to help you reach your ideal tomorrow? I've talked a lot about releasing expectation and being more in the journey because it is key to the healing process. Let's take it one step deeper; welcome to the art of becoming. It is a journey into "the now," which becomes an adventure of creativity, curiosity, awareness, and self-respect. In this space, you create a platform for self-love and compassion. My art of becoming is a forever experience. Because our full potential is life itself. As long as we are trying and doing the best we know how, that is enough.

I teach writing, public speaking, and advertising classes part-time at the Art Institute of Portland, and the first day of every class I tell students I don't grade on talent or skill. I don't care how you compare with the student next to you; I grade you on your own potential and whether you are giving it the best effort you possibly can. This always catches a few students off guard. There are some students who are insanely talented with certain graphic design skills, yet they have slacked off. In my classes I push them to explore new areas of their skill set and go beyond what is comfortable. Then there are other students who are still timid around graphic programs or afraid to write their copy and feature articles, and I encourage them to move beyond fear and try, just try. Both students will get an A if they try their best and push beyond their known limits. It comes back to the effort we put into life. There is always a student each term who constantly comes in late, doesn't turn in the homework, and won't participate in class; this does not show an effort, and to me these students are not in the process of becoming. This student is checked out of school for whatever reason, but I remind my students that how you are in here is how you are in life. There is no separation between getting into the real world and your "real world" today. Many students think school is just a rehearsal; they will just do the work, the bare minimum, but not be fully present because they are so focused on getting a job in their chosen field. We do this in our adult life, too. We want to be at that goal weight so much, or in that relationship, or debt free, or in the job we love so badly, that we bypass or do the bare minimum in the moment because our attention is on tomorrow. If you want to be rewarded in life, you have to give yourself permission to show up more fully in the present. The now matters, and the art of becoming is the adventure of life that leads to the outcome you truly desire. Just like my A students, the effort you put in now, the potential you pursue now, makes life more wonderful.

At some point on our Self-Love Experiment journey, we have to just let go and jump in. What does this mean? It means stop trying to figure it out and dive in to deepen your own life adventure. It means going into each situation and moment and feeling it fully. Allow what needs to come up to come up. When I did this, I saw that there is real, uninhibited, glorious beauty in our breakdowns. This means that everything we are experiencing is part of a bigger plan, and you will have moments where you feel as though you aren't moving ahead. Maybe you will feel stuck or as if your efforts don't equal the results you want to see. When this happens, realize you are more on track than you can imagine. This is the art of becoming but also what I call beauty in the breakdown. All of it—the setbacks, insecurities, failures—they are all designed to help us dive into life fully, embracing it as much as possible. Beauty in the breakdown means you know that

What you are going through is part of a bigger life plan.

I use to self-flagellate because I overate yet again; the weight on the scale wasn't going down, and I was frustrated and extremely angry with myself. Yet another day had gone by and I felt off track. Then something happened that changed everything for me—I dove deep into my emotions, and I let go. My inner voice, which sounded kind of like an authority chiming in from the heaven, said, "You are right where you need to be. All of this is by design."

My mind flashed to images of me teaching others about self-love and helping people fall in love with themselves. I saw that my breakdown was part of a bigger plan, a universal calling that by some strange, odd turn of events made me see the magnitude of my pain. If there was purpose to all of my pain, then I could let go of feeling like I was off track. All of what I was experiencing was as it should be. The same goes for you; all of what you are experiencing is as it should be, it is part of a bigger plan for you.

Breakdowns, emotional setbacks, fear, frustration—they are all part of being human. When we run from these depths and feel as if we aren't supposed to experience them, this causes catastrophic repercussions. Instead, dive in; it can be amazing, truly, when you allow yourself to go to the depths of your emotional capacity. Let yourself cry, hurt, feel. Because in these moments of breakdown you will find the real beauty, you will find your truth.

It's important to remember that what you want, wants you, too.

As I was working toward a more balanced, healthy life, I knew in my heart that my body also wanted what I did, to be loved, respected, and cherished, to be healthy and in shape. Everything in our life that happens is the direct result of our energy and its alignment. What we focus on, we become. This is why for years, when I felt ugly and fat, my body gained weight and manifested itself into what I was focusing on. Once I adopted the Self-Love Experiment and discovered compassion and self-respect, my energy started to feel more uplifting and light filled. I felt more aligned with my true self, and I felt beautiful and happy. Life was much more manageable. But here is why it was easier: I was in an energetic alignment with my true desire and core wish.

Esther and Jerry Hicks share the teaching of Abraham, which is the foundation of the law of attraction, and in their teaching they say:

> There are only two states to be in. What is wanted and the absence of what is wanted.

Meaning you might want something but it isn't happening, so you are more focused on how it isn't coming true or on what isn't working. This means there is an active vibration that is holding what you really want out at arm's length, holding it away from you. In order to manifest what you really want, you must align your energy to your desire. This means you act and behave as if it is already here. Once I identified that I wanted a relationship with a man and I was ready to fall in love, I stopped feeling lonely, and I stopped focusing on how I was single. Instead, I felt loved and cared for because I was showing up for me. In this experience I could meet potential suitors much more easily. The same goes for anything you want in your life. If you are more focused on how it isn't here, then it will just stay outside of your reach. But shifting your attention to the vibration and energetic alignment of how it feels to have that which you desire in your life is the key to it manifesting.

Most of us focus on what isn't going well. We spend years, decades even, focusing on our flaws and frustrations. But our attention to the problem keeps the problem front and center. In order to shift our awareness, we need to focus on the good. I call this "grasp the good." I found good things about me, and when I discovered self-love, my attention and focus on my problems disappeared.

When you stop focusing on the problem, the problem goes away.

As I write this book, I share that there are no problems. My body is not an issue; in fact I love it dearly and celebrate its beauty. How did I arrive here? I focused on being in energetic alignment. If you are still struggling with an area of your life, an insecurity or flaw, do everything in your power to stop focusing on that situation. Instead, turn your attention to what is going well in your life. I did this by looking at the pieces of my life I loved. I *love* my career. I get to work and play from anywhere in the world, and with great gratitude I am thrilled I get to write and be a teacher helping people find their own truth. This is my calling. So I tried this theory with the areas I was struggling with, like accepting myself, and I took all of my attention off my weight and insecurity. If people talked about diets I didn't chime in; instead I focused all my attention on what was going well in my life—my career, my love of life, my travels— and this energy was infectious. It spread into the areas that I used to feel a lack in. All of a sudden I felt more at peace in my body and in my romantic life and started to go out and meet more people and date again. Things flourished for me because I was in energetic alignment to my true needs and desires. When we stop tunnel visioning the problems in our lives, the problems can work themselves out. You will feel more peace and joy. What problem are you obsessing over? Can you turn your attention to the good? Grasp the good, focus on what is going well in your life, do everything in your power to stop thinking about the problems, and as you turn your attention away, they, too, will go away.

You have to be an active participant in attracting what you really want. So stop focusing on the flaws or things you dislike and tunnel vision yourself into looking only at what is going well. The law of attraction will play in your favor when you choose to align with the energetic vibration of goodness and joy. Your only mission is to focus on the good, grasp the good. This will lead you to your epiphany and breakthrough.

We all want it, we try for it, we read self-help books, attend courses, talk to friends, we try, try, try to reach that solution. The glorious aha moment: brilliance seemingly strikes out of nowhere, and instantly we have it all figured out. Hello, epiphany! I've been waiting for you. Most of us have had moments of realizations, whether it's suddenly seeing your significant others without rose-colored glasses, or the gut-wrenching aha moment when you realize you hate your job but it's all you know how to do.

> Epiphanies are mental moments when we have instant clarity—they inspire and motivate us to charge forward and change the aspects of our lives we find unfulfilling.

But not all epiphanies are created equally. Some demand a deep inward search, and you'll be stuck asking the tough questions to see what you are made of. Other times they fly in and out of our lives swiftly, silently, almost unseen. Many of my coaching clients first come to me looking for the epiphany—that instant moment when you have it figured out and all the emotional pain is wiped away with clarity. It often happens for them. Excited, they return and say, "I had my aha moment!"

It's great to have an epiphany, but what you do with that new clarity is what matters most. Most of our habits are so ingrained in our life that changing our behaviors can be challenging. Yet our epiphanies force us to see situations and ourselves in a new light.

What is required, then, is courage. And taking that step to live out your epiphany is when real transformation happens. In my own life the epiphany came when I released the shame and guilt associated with myself. I stopped apologizing for my desires and needs or how I looked. What happened was freedom. I felt alive and excited to be true to my real self.

The important thing is to stop!

Stop trying to reach your aha moment. Let it happen.

Stop trying to reach self-love. Let it happen.

Stop apologizing for what you want or how you look and feel.

Stop trying to find romantic love. Let it happen.

Stop chasing your dreams. Let them come to you.

The glorious aha moment will come when you stop trying to figure it all out. You've heard women say they found the love of their lives when "they weren't even looking." Well, this is the same concept.

When we stop obsessing and focusing
so much on what we want, what we
want can come to us.

Once I stopped focusing on the number on the scale and obsessing over food, I naturally lost weight, more than twenty pounds, because I was focusing on joy and love. I stopped trying to find the big epiphany and instead started to live my life more passionately.

When the aha moment comes to you, apply it to your life. Instead of being a passive bystander, standing on the outskirts of your life, dive in fully and embrace each moment. Epiphanies come in all shapes and sizes, but certain ones we can realize sooner rather than later. Epiphanies are moments of clarity that help us realign with our authentic selves. When you hear something that makes sense, it rings true at the core of your being. Your life has forever been changed.

179

> ## A real epiphany creates transformation. You can no longer return to the person you were before you discovered it.

But the power is in the practice. You must practice the new information and integrate it into your daily routine. My epiphany with self-love was realizing that there is nothing wrong with me. I don't have to be fixed. So I am a chubby girl living in a world that praises skinny. That doesn't make me ugly, wrong, or unlovable. The goal is to achieve balance with your true self, not with what others think is best for you or with what the world says is ideal. Align yourself with your heart's center, and the reward is living a life you are in love with. You honor the rhythm of your own soul.

Put your epiphanies into practice. These are eight epiphanies I discovered in my own Self-Love Experiment. They have certainly changed my life for the better, and maybe they can help you, too.

Eight epiphanies everyone should have

1. You aren't what people say you are.

What matters most is what you say and feel about yourself. You get to choose; you can let others define you and tell you who you are, or you can show them who you are. Be you. The world needs you as you are.

2. Plan B is often better than Plan A.

The most freeing moment in your life is when you let go of what you think is best for you and allow the universe to show you what you really need. Stop holding on to what is no longer working: that job, that relationship, that dream. If it feels like hard work and is causing you more pain than gain, it is time to release it. Instead, follow your heart.

3. You are not the number on the scale.

At the end of your life, the weight struggles, the food wars, or the obsession with new diets and trying to look a certain way will have no relevance. The only thing that matters is what is in your heart. How you make people feel and how you make *you* feel are more important than how you look.

4. The journey is more important than the goal.

Yes, reaching goals is important, but the actual process of becoming, growing, learning, and morphing into who we need to become is the real sweet stuff that makes a wonderful life. Enjoy the journey as much as the reward.

5. Being alone doesn't mean you will be lonely.

The fear of being alone strikes the heart and makes many people settle. But when you learn to love your own company, you will see that you are never really lonely.

6. It will never be all done.

The to-do lists, the chores, the things we race around to get done, will never be done. It is called life. Situations, chores, and to-do lists will always unfold. Instead of focusing on the end result, be in the process and celebrate what you have accomplished.

7. Emotional pain shows up to help us know what we need to change.

Sadness, depression, and heartache are gentle reminders to probe deeper into our lives. Look at what is not working and be open to living your life in new ways. You will see that one day it will all make sense.

8. You don't have to find your purpose; it will find you.

The transition period between who you were and where you are going can be painful. But during your journey of finding purpose, recognize that there is purpose in the pain. Each step you take is helping you carve out more of how you really are. Instead of regretting or resisting, try turning inward and embracing the journey into joy.

We all get tied up in trying to control certain areas of our life, and we become obsessed with the outcome. Perhaps you worry about when you will find a boyfriend. Or maybe you're trying to control the result of a project at work. We all have personal ways we fall into when worrying about an outcome, which makes us try to control the outcome.

What I learned in my experiment is that there is always a solution of the highest good happening on your behalf. It may not be what you think is best for you, but:

182

We may not always get what we want, but we will always get what we need.

If things aren't going the way you planned or you aren't seeing the outcome clearly, the real question becomes how we remain hopeful when the outcome is uncertain. By knowing that the universe is working on a plan greater than yours and everything that happens is always for your highest good, you can relax a little more into the natural rhythm of your life.

Maybe you haven't seen the results you want, but don't worry about what is going on currently. Focus all your attention on what you want. Release the need to have it look an exact way, and instead focus your energy on the results you want to see. When you focus on what you want, the rejection along the way will not faze you, because you aren't attached to the outcome—instead, you trust that the right pieces will align. If you commit yourself to putting all your focus on what you want, you will get it much faster. It's important to trust the timing of our dreams. There is timing to our desires being realized.

APPRECIATE THE UNKNOWN AND THE SPACE IN BETWEEN

Everything happens at the right time and in the right place.

A huge part of turning the uncertainty into certainty in your life is to trust that everything has a universal timing. I may think I know when my next book should be out, but the universe always has a greater plan. I may think I know when I want to find my soul mate, but the universe always has a plan greater than ours. It's important to remember you can't make a mistake when it comes to your life and living your authentic truth. All is always in right order and nothing is out of place. During my experiment, when I started to worry about being single and wonder if I would ever find love, I would repeat the mantra "You are not off track; you cannot make a mistake. What is right and meant for you will come at the right time."

If you wish something would happen that has yet to manifest itself, recognize that there is a divine timing to your dreams coming true. Plus you are still becoming who you need to be in order to live out that dream.

Remember: what you want, wants you, too, and believing in your dream, believing in you, and knowing everything in life happens for your highest good will help you feel more balanced and cared for.

You are not off track, you cannot make a mistake. What is right and meant for you will always come at the right time.

#MeMattersMantra

You must try . . . not because

you'll regret it if you don't,

but because you haven't even

scratched the surface of all

you're capable of.

—ANONYMOUS

PART 5

ME MATTERS

Show Up for Yourself

Show Up for Your Body

OUR BODY IS THE most important vessel to care for when it comes to living a fulfilled life. Through my own Self-Love Experiment my relationship with my body radically changed, and as you start to care for your body, loving it becomes natural. Today my life looks a lot different than it did before my Self-Love Experiment. Now I read all ingredient labels, I mostly avoid sugar, and I can eat one or two bites of ice cream and be done. My body craves movement and healthful, organic foods; I no longer obsess or worry about food but instead live and enjoy my life fully. And most important, I treat myself with respect and love. One of the ways I was able to do this was to align with body-confident role models. Find people who have what you want. Think of people either in the public eye or your own circle of friends who have a positive relationship with food and talk kindly about themselves.

Aligning yourself with more positive, body-confident people will make it easier for you to establish a solid relationship with your own body. Think of positive people who inspire us to love ourselves and our bodies. For example, singer-songwriter Meghan

Trainor is widely known for her popular pop song "All About That Bass," which inspires women to accept how they were born. In 2016 she debuted a new music video, "Me Too," but much to her fans' surprise, the video was quickly taken down. Later she took to her Snapchat account to explain why her video disappeared: the ridiculous Photoshop retouches had changed her body too much. She is proud of who she is and how she looks and stood by the message that we are beautiful as we are. Accept your body as it is because it is a beautiful vessel of love.

One of the biggest barriers to accepting our body is our negative thoughts about it. Most of us spend so much time emotionally beating ourselves up and blaming our bodies for the problems in our life. Remember, we cannot hate ourselves into changing.

> Negative energy cannot remove hate.
> In order to remove negative things we
> must send love, we must love them.

But the good news is the body is quick to forgive. When you are kind to your body and treat it with respect, it will transform. I have lost almost twenty-five pounds without really trying since the start of my own experiment. I realized I needed to become what I wanted to attract. If you really want to create positive transformation in your life:

> You have to become what you
> want to attract.

If you want to meet a romantic partner who is healthy, you need to be that for yourself. If you want an abundant business and a successful career, you need to care for yourself first. If you want to fulfill your dreams, then caring for your body is the most essential ingredient to do this. Because we can't live our dreams if our body is breaking down. When we drop our guard and stop fighting against ourselves, we will find peace.

Peace prevails when we stop resisting and fighting against what is.

Self-love starts with being willing to heal. Not from a place of hate, frustration, or desperation, but from a place of gentle compassion, joy, and love. And healing starts with a single step, one small step at a time. It requires us to step outside of our comfort zone and do what we have yet to try. We need to go beyond the safety net of what we have settled and conditioned ourselves to live. It means showing up and being committed to feeling radiant and healthy and letting that desire to feel good be your sole responsibility and dedicated focus. You owe it to yourself to love yourself, and in the experience of caring for your body, your entire world will change.

I AM AT PEACE IN MY BODY. ALL IS WELL.

#MeMattersMantra

Show Up for the Experience

ELF-LOVE IS LAYERED, AND it isn't about just caring for your body and treating yourself well but is also about showing up for your mind, too. Essentially, it starts in the mind. If you've noticed a theme throughout my experiment, it is that how we talk to ourselves matters. What you say to yourself is not only important but also essential to a happy life. I showed up for myself by not only addressing my inner critic but also by showing up for my mind in new ways. One of my driving needs is learning. A driving need is a core attribute that you need as a person to feel whole and complete. When your driving needs are expressed, you feel balanced. When I am not learning and growing I feel like something is off. If you love to learn new things, then the Self-Love Experiment is a great opportunity to show up for your mind. Part of being in the Self-Love Experiment is a deep lesson in learning about your own self and true needs.

As I mentioned, the process of writing this book felt challenging at times. I was like a workhorse, forcing myself to write the pages, because resistance kept coming up. "What if you write the entire book and a publisher doesn't buy it? You've just written more than sixty thousand words—what is it all for?" my ego would scream out.

My writer self said, "This is the writer's life, and you show up for yourself." But something happened during the process. I felt like I was forcing it and the work was too hard. I chose to be a writer so I could express myself and be free. I wanted to creatively have fun, but it felt like a chore. And then it clicked: sometimes our passion is a process. We have to work at our goals and commit to them daily. The road isn't smooth and paved with perfect sceneries, and there is no cookie cutter to anything. Every goal requires a new dedication from us, a new aspect to show up, a part of us that we may have previously been unaware of. This works two ways. If you've tried to reach a goal before and it has yet to be achieved, that means there is a new part of you ready to show up and try it again. We are always changing and growing and becoming more of who we really need to be, so allowing yourself to be where you are and learning the steps along the way will help you reach freedom. As my business coach, Marie Forleo, says, "Everything is figurable." This means you can and will find a way to make it happen, but you have to take action steps.

Also remember you are more you today than you were yesterday. Every day we learn and grow and get more pieces to the life puzzle, so each day is an opportunity to move forward with more grace and ease. You may feel off track, but you were never on a track.

Consider that life is a giant adventure, the greatest one you will ever have.

And as in real-life adventures, we sometimes are unsure, we aren't always confident, and things aren't always perfect. My dear friend Alison Leipzig, co-founder of Soul Camp and a self-love coach, wrote this in her newsletter. They are powerful words on this topic:

There's this myth that you have to love every piece of yourself in order to experience self-love. That you need to love every inch of your body in order to have body confidence.

But there's harm that comes with that line of thinking. We can fall into a deadly trap of self-denial when we are expecting to love every piece of ourselves. We become afraid to look at the ways we show up in our lives. We are afraid to see parts of ourselves that aren't so beautiful. We are afraid to accept the fact that we gained thirty pounds. We don't want to admit that we are oftentimes self-centered or critical of others. Or that we can be spoiled and short-tempered. Whatever it is, we don't look at it. Instead, we project it onto the people around us. They did this to me, they are so critical, they are incredibly judgmental. Well, how are you all of those things as well?

195

Self-acceptance requires radical, courageous honesty.

And when you aim for self-acceptance, it brings an unshakable power. Because when you know who you are, no one can take away your power. You will feel sad. You will feel anger. You will feel hurt, of course. But you won't be taken down. You will rise. You will thrive. You will use those situations to help you get back up again.

We are all looking to feel whole. What we don't realize is we are already whole right now—but this includes our "flaws." If we deny parts of ourselves that are less than ideal, we will never realize true wholeness.

Accept yourself as you are in all of your beautiful wholeness. In my own journey, I stopped thinking about outcomes, how this story would end—Would I find self-love? (yes, I did); Would I find romantic love? (I believe I found the greatest love of my life, with myself); Would I lose weight? (yes)—I released it all, the worry is gone. As I surrendered and let go, I let myself be more in the journey. The outcome no longer mattered. It was the process that was unfolding. And the outcome, my dear friend, turned out to be even more beautiful than I could have ever imagined because I was fully present in the experience. Why? Because I let go and surrendered fully to the journey. This is the magic of the Self-Love Experiment.

I accept myself as
I AM WHOLE
and complete in my
AUTHENTIC
TRUTH.

#MeMattersMantra

Show Up for Your Doubts

*I*N 2009, WHEN MY doctor diagnosed me with clinical depression, I was living my life from my head. My rational mind was making all the choices. Get a good job, find a man you can settle down with, graduate with honors, check, check, check. I was going through the motions but didn't feel connected to my life. At the time, I was also suffering from eating disorders and drug addictions, and I hated my job in advertising. The problem was that I didn't know how to break free. I shuffled my way through life, masking the pain with addictions, fear, and self-sabotage. I had the sinking sensation my corporate cubicle lifestyle—despite putting myself through graduate school to get this high-profile job—was not my life purpose. It didn't bring me joy, and I didn't feel passionate about it.

That's the thing about most major life choices: we don't know how they will fit in our life plan until we try them out. I thought I wanted that life. I participated fully in every moment to create that reality. But once I achieved it, I felt numb, hollow, and uninspired.

When my inner voice told me to "follow your heart," everything changed for me. I dropped from my mind, the doubtful, fearful part of us, and into my heart. I redirected and removed what no longer served me, including my corporate job, drug addictions, eating disorders, and attachment to fear and the relationship that no longer worked.

Instead of focusing on my pain, I began to focus on my passions, which led me to my purpose. Today I lead a much happier, healthier life because I stepped through my doubts.

Happiness is a habit, and I do what I love every day because I listen to my heart. I've learned to cultivate this as a habit.

It may be scary at first to leave a situation that is suffocating your soul, but your future self knows it's worth it. Your life depends on your courage and stepping into your true passion to live a purposeful life. You don't need an insane amount of courage to follow your heart. You just need to believe in yourself, and that comes when you take action. What I learned along my journey is the more we focus on trying to "find" our life purpose or self-love, or answers to our pain, or figure out a fix for our situation, the harder it is to reach. This is because we try to think our way into it, when the best solution is to actually *feel* our way.

149

Drop from your head into your heart and allow it to be your compass. Your life will open up to tremendous new ways and possibilities, and inspiration and love will guide you forward. You will feel joy from the inside out. With your heart as your compass, things become more peaceful.

Your heart is intimately connected to your intuition, whereas your head is connected to your fear. How do you know the difference between intuition and fear? Or, otherwise put, how do you know if you are making the right choice? On our journey to living life fully we often brush up against the emotional walls that demarcate our "comfort zone," especially when we long for something more than we currently have.

Recognize that right before a breakthrough there is usually a surge of insecurity, self-doubt, and fear. This is why sometimes things get worse before they get better. Jumping from one stage of your life into the next can be nerve-racking, especially if you don't know if it's fear or intuition in the driver's seat. I remember when fear kept me paralyzed and in a corporate job I stayed in long past its expiration date. It wasn't until I recognized the difference between fear and intuition that I saw the powerful potential of releasing the fear in order to access my dreams.

The thing about our doubts and insecurities is that they are manifestations of fear. That's it. As related in the life-changing book *A Course in Miracles,* all fear is false. We verify this when we step out of our comfort zone and suddenly our fears disappear. Fear goes away as soon as you step up and address it. This is what showing up for our doubts really means.

Our doubts are indicators, leading us into deeper awareness of our true needs and our deepest truth.

During my Self-Love Experiment, I came to realize that I had a choice: to stay still and let fear win, or to dive straight in. I chose the latter. What happens when we start to love ourselves and show up more fully for our life is that fear no longer has a playground to jump around in. It's new for us to love ourselves, and anything new brings up fears of the unknown. So fear naturally will get louder when you are closer to greatness and reaching your goals. For me, I addressed my fear head-on. I said, I know you are here, but you are not going to have any say. You can be here for the party, but love is making choices. By addressing my fear head-on, I was practicing self-love.

Standing up to your doubts and fears takes courage. It takes a dedication and willingness to rise up and say, "I am worth it," and "Love will conquer." But our insecurities are deep-rooted. For many of us they go back to childhood, and if you believe in past lives, they can even circle back to lifetimes ago.

The thing about doubt is that it can be quite useful if we use it as a means to discovering insecure feelings that need to be addressed.

During my Self-Love Experiment, when I lived overseas I traveled with a group of people on an African tour. I was traveling with strangers soon to be friends, and this experience in itself brought up my unhealed insecurities. The first few days we all met were really awkward and felt a little forced. The group was finding its footing. There was one girl who really didn't seem to like or want to talk to me. I noticed her making some side comments, and I felt incredibly judged by her. I saw her as "the cool girl," as she seemed to get along with the "pretty girls" and "popular boys." Here I was in my midthirties, feeling like I was in junior high again. Her ignoring me, whether she did it on purpose or not, brought me right back to my childhood, where I always felt as if I was on the outside looking in. I always felt like I was just not quite with the in crowd, and this kept me separated. I felt different, odd, funny, and like an outcast.

The travel trip I took as an adult brought up all my insecurities that I had failed to address as a child. Luckily for me, I was deep into my Self-Love Experiment during this trip and I chose to look at my doubts instead of feeling like a victim or running away from them. I first addressed my doubts of feeling unworthy and like an outsider and asked myself, "Where does this come from? What is the root cause?" I realized the same feeling of being left out was traced back to when I was young and moved to a new school. As a child, I moved a lot because my parents took new jobs in different cities and states, and I was always the new girl. I always took a while to settle in and feel like I fit, but in reality I never felt like I fit. I was often bullied and made fun of because I was the new person in the class. When I addressed this doubt as an adult, I started to see that fitting in was not all it was cracked up to be. I thought to myself, "I don't really need to fit in. This is just a group I am traveling with, not my new BFFs." I said to myself, "I don't need them to like me, because I like me!"

Most of us find ourselves in situations that may make us uncomfortable or insecure. Often it is because of a childhood issue that has not been addressed or healed. Something happened when you were a child and the fear continues to play out as an adult. Ask yourself, "Where does this come from? What is the root cause?"

After a few days I realized that I didn't really care if that girl didn't like me and was ignoring me. I don't need her to like me for me to "be cool." Our perception is our reality. And I changed my perception from "I feel like an outsider and don't fit in" to "I love myself, and I am enough as I am." This is a powerful self-love practice, to change your perception by addressing your doubts head-on. As you do this you will relate to the world from a place of power. You see, I didn't need her to like me because I liked myself. But before my Self-Love Experiment, I would have felt insecure the entire trip and needed her approval to feel okay about myself.

A few days after I had my realization that I am enough and am not really an outsider (I just felt that way because I wasn't addressing my fears or insecurities), the woman who I thought didn't like me pulled me aside. She said to me, "I don't know if you know this, but when we first met I was really intimidated by you. I thought you represented something I don't know much about, you seem to have it all together, you are happy and successful, you are the whole package." She went on to say she felt stuck in life and lost and didn't know how to be around someone who actually felt good about themselves and life. She had been feeling insecure and intimidated just as I was—both of us had had perceptions about each other that were based on past doubts and fears.

Once we addressed them and actually worked through them, we were able to become friends. This is what showing up for your doubts and fears truly means, because loving yourself also means loving your fears. Give yourself permission to be present with whatever comes up in each situation. Instead of feeling intimidated or like you are stuck, simply ask, "What would love do?" I worked though my own insecurities by asking this. As you start to show up for your doubts, you may feel the need to show up more for your inner child. I certainly did.

203

My doubts are just manifested fears that need **MORE LOVE AND ATTENTION.**

Show Up for Your Inner Child

THROUGH MY COACHING PRACTICE and almost a decade of teaching, I've discovered most of us have a piece of ourselves that we left back in our childhood. It is a part that as adults we may ignore or leave in the shadows without much thought, but it is the piece of us that needs attention and care. It is tied to our beliefs about ourselves and how we see the world. For example, I always felt as though I didn't fit in, so as an adult I still felt like I was on the outside looking in—until I found self-love, of course—whereas my friend I told you about in the last section felt intimidated by successful people. Both of these are childhood wounds that were never addressed or cared for. So for a moment let's go back into our past. The little us, the little dreamers, the little doers, the little believers and achievers who want to do good but sometimes feel like the world is out to get us and we can't do anything right.

This is a fear that started in our childhood. Think about your biggest insecurity and the fear that is holding you back. Then trace back to your childhood a time when this happened, maybe the first time you felt this insecurity. Usually our fears start when we are young. Everything is going fine, we are happy, comfortable, we feel safe and free. Then, without much warning, something seemingly out of the blue happens. Dad loses his job and you have to move, or your parents get a divorce, or a family member dies, or we witness something unexpected that shakes us to our core—a situation happens that alters our reality. We no longer feel safe or happy; we go into protection mode. We build walls and shut down. Many of us emotionally, physically, and spiritually shut down. We learn to relate to the world in a new way. We become a half version of ourselves in order to protect ourselves from experiencing that horrible situation ever again.

In order to really feel peace with ourselves, we have to be able to give ourselves what others never did.

This is what I discovered on my own Self-Love Experiment. That a piece of me was still left behind. My nine-year-old self, the one who just arrived at a new school and went for a special physical education day and couldn't finish the mile. All the other students laughed at me and started calling me names. The movie *Free Willy*, about the orca whale, had just come out, and some of the kids started yelling, "Free Willy." Kids can be mean, but no one is as mean as ourselves. I felt abandoned, misunderstood, ugly, and fat. And I came home and my parents were both at work and not there, so I felt unloved and turned to food. Food became my crutch and only source of comfort. Thus my insecurity with my body started as a result of my feeling unloved and out of place. As I grew older, there was still a little nine-year-old girl who needed love and care. Through my Self-Love Experiment I learned the power of returning to my true self. That little girl is a piece of me, she is wounded, she needs love, and she needs care.

As I paid more attention to the piece of me that felt left behind, I started to awaken to possibilities for myself. Instead of feeling sorry for myself or as if I were on the outside looking in, I started to change my focus and saw myself through a loving lens. I paid more attention to the inner child within me. The inner child in us has needs and desires. If we want to be happy, we have to listen to our inner child and see that child. My inner child loves to play; the little me wants more joy in my life. What does your inner child need? Showing up for your inner child means showing up for your true desires and giving yourself more attention and care.

As the saying goes, sometimes we must be lost in order to be found. During my Self-Love Experiment, I was lost in life. Nothing was really off on the outside, but I felt it on the inside. Instead of fearing this feeling, I dove into the situation and asked, "What can this feeling teach me? What is it trying to show me?" My feeling of being off track was an awakening to live my life in new ways. More expansive ways. Ways that make me feel connected to my best self.

This desire was a need of mine that my inner child craved for me. She wants me to be happy, secure, and free; my inner child wants me to be in joy and shining bright. So through my experiment I gave her full permission to show up more fully, by giving in to her needs. It is all connected—your true desires, your needs, and your fears from your past.

When you love yourself, you send love
to the parts of you that were hurt in
the past and it is then easier to heal.

Let yourself be moved by your own courage and show up for your inner child. I did, and it changed my world. Literally, I am writing this book while I am living my dream, living in Morocco for a month. I am able to do that because I said yes to my dreams, yes to my inner child, and yes to loving me.

I AM
the person
I NEEDED
when
I was younger.

#MeMattersMantra

Show Up for Your Dreams

a **BIG PART OF LOVING** yourself is showing up for yourself, which means showing up for your desires. We all have dreams that come to us, and they come to us for a reason. Your job is to tune in and trust them.

> Your dreams are the invisible
> architecture of your life.
> Trust them. Honor them.

They come to you because they are part of your destiny—your calling, if you will. Imagine there is a special life-force inside of you that comes to you because you are the person to actualize it. Your dreams are this life-force in action. My dream to become a writer was part of my calling and life plan. Imagine if I had ignored that nudge. I am a big believer in believing in yourself, and you do this by trusting your heart and the dreams that come to you. Martha Graham said it best:

There is a vitality, a life-force, an energy . . . that is translated through you into action and because there is only one of you in all of time, this expression is unique. . . . It is not your business to determine how good it is . . . it is your business . . . to keep the channel open.[18]

Here's the thing you have to know: your uniqueness is your gift. The dreams you have are your gift to the world. When you are living with the full integrity of your purpose, you inspire others. It is not your job to determine how people will take it; all you have to commit to is honoring the dreams by actualizing them. This is the true beauty of the Self-Love Experiment. It is knowing that your heart is your compass for a satisfying, rich, rewarding life. Everything you need is inside of you. Fulfillment isn't some outward goal achieved, but it is honoring the wisdom and soft whisper within. Listening to the voice and knowing that you are showing up fully and doing the best you can is a real achievement. That is the real magic of self-love. The dreams you have come to you because you, my dear, are the best person in the entire world to live them. So trust them, honor them, nurture them. You owe it to yourself, and in turn you will uplift and help everyone around you.

Instead of asking yourself, "How can I reach self-love?", ask, "How can I follow my heart?", for once you have truly honored your heart's pull, you will love yourself.

I spoke to one of my dear friends the other day, and she was sharing that she is being asked to expand her business and stop one-on-one coaching and move to more speaking and group settings so she can impact more people. She's been a coach for many years and is terrified of releasing that part of her business, but at the same time she knows it is the very thing she needs to do to step fully into her power and own her authentic truth. Even though it is scary, the release is where she will find freedom.

Change is part of the process; we have to invite it into our lives because it is the only constant. My friend said to me, "I have what I wanted. I first left my corporate job three years ago to create my own business, and I am living today that life I set out to create. I've arrived, but my soul is yearning for more now. The question becomes, now what?" As she shared, I realized we are always growing more into who we really are. We set out to make goals, and when we reach them, we become a newer version of ourselves.

We reach for new dreams, new ones that were left undone, and our past predictions about achievements are manifested. Our dreams, our desires, they change, they morph, they grow.

As we grow, our desires change and grow.

Your power is not in the dreams but in allowing yourself to grow and change with them. Most of us put ourselves into boxes. We fall into routines; safe, comfortable habits become the thread of our daily worry. The yearning, the pull of the desire in our hearts, comes to us for a reason. Most of us stay in the box. We stick to a routine, we fall into societal expectations, and we pat ourselves on the back for following the rules, but on the inside we are crying. Our hearts want more, need more; our hearts have messages, and

211

if you listen to your heart, it will always lead you to fulfillment. Break out of your box, which means stop trying to fit into society's expectations of you, and instead invite the world to fit to you.

The goals in your heart are part of your self-expression. You owe it to yourself to go for it. And when you do, you will never look back. You will understand the true value of self-love, because you will be an example of what is possible when you live your life in full integrity and alignment with you. So, dear one, please break out of your box. What is it in your heart you've always wanted to do? Go for it. Now is the time.

MY HEART KNOWS WHAT MY HEAD HAS YET TO FIGURE OUT. I TRUST IT.

#MeMattersMantra

Show Up for Joy

*J*OY IS THE HIGHEST form of self-love. When we are joyous, we are fully alive. Doing what brings you joy and making sure you feel joy daily is true self-love. I learned this in my own experiment. Before my experiment I was happy but not fully in joy. Joy is pure bliss and excitement; happy is an expression, but it can come and go. We aim to be happy because we think it will bring us joy, but I learned in order to reach happiness we must truly tap into joy. Joy became my full-time mission. I surrounded myself with positive people I already had in my life and met new friends who were happy. Joy was the leading force in my life. I made a list of all the things that brought me joy. Things I loved to do and things that helped me feel like my best self. As I started to show up for joy, my life transformed. Things that I once did by habit, such as mindlessly eating in front of the TV, no longer brought me any joy whatsoever. I canceled my cable and cleared out my cupboards. I found joy in new online courses and in watching documentaries or travel shows. I started to fill up my joy tank by addressing my needs daily. I asked myself, "What do I need to be happy?" As it turned out, it wasn't a lot. Good food, family, and friends. Traveling. A day spent writing. Playing in nature and moving my body with a hike or nature walk. Exploring new places. I began to have pretty good days indeed. This was my new joy route. A joy route is like following your bliss, and as Joseph Campbell said, to be happy we must follow our bliss.

Here's a secret about being happy that no one talks about. You can be happy but not be in joy. It seems to me it is more important to strive for joy than to reach for happiness. Joy is the best barometer for success, too. If you want to gauge how successful you are in your work, in your relationship, in any aspect of your life, then ask yourself, "How much joy do I feel?" I did this during my Self-Love Experiment, and at the start of it, I was appalled at my answer. I was not living in joy at all. I was settling, I was overweight, my body hurt, I was lonely and wasn't taking care of myself. I was just going through the motions, just scraping by. Each day, it felt like a chore to make it through. I would go to bed each night saying to myself, "Tomorrow is a new day; you can always try better and start again." Then day after day things never improved until I committed and actually focused on joy. Joy became my full-time mission. I made joy my intention, and setting joy as a goal helped me attain self-love.

Joy is the entry point for self-love.
The more joy you allow in your life,
the easier it is to love yourself.

I wanted to feel joy, and soon enough my life transformed. I felt more joy in all areas of my life. Now it's your turn: How can you show up for joy?

Joy is the best
barometer for
happiness.
THE MORE
JOY I FEEL,
THE HAPPIER I AM.

#MeMattersMantra

Show Up for Yourself

DO YOU EVER FEEL tired from being there for everyone else and not having enough time for you? I work with a coaching client who had a blog for mamas, and her main focus was helping moms take time out for themselves. Interestingly, this was something she struggled with herself, and so the blog was not only a way for her to reach other people and form a community but also a way to hold herself accountable for carving out self-love time. In our last session, she expressed her frustration with feeling exhausted after every day. We identified that her emotional lows were directly tied to her overgiving to everyone else but not taking time out for herself. This is a common situation for mothers, but you don't have to be a mom to be an overgiver. If you are tired all the time and always there for other people but don't show up for yourself, you might be an overgiver. Women especially (though some men, too, including many men I have worked with in my coaching practice and workshops) are natural givers. We give life, time, love, energy, creativity, even ourselves. We naturally put the needs of others before ourselves. It's a quality that comes naturally to most people with big hearts. Sadly, what is hard for these bighearted people is that it is truly hard for them to receive.

We give, give, give, give, and that leaves us depleted. The fix: open up to receiving! You deserve to find the balance and fulfillment that comes from receiving.

Receiving isn't easy. If it were, more of us would do it with grace and gratitude. Is there a way to change that? I believe so. I've seen many clients successfully go from overworked overgivers to graceful receivers.

But how? First we have to look at our beliefs around receiving. Common limiting beliefs I see (and had myself) are:

* You feel as though it is selfish to get what you want.
* You feel as though there isn't enough to go around (enough money, enough food, enough resources, enough time, etc.).
* You feel as though you matter only when you help others.
* You don't feel deserving of what you desire.
* Others' needs are more important than your own.

Ask yourself if you relate to any of these.

I love the book *The Power of Receiving: A Revolutionary Approach to Giving Yourself the Life You Want and Deserve* by Amanda Owen. The author says that women especially are reluctant to embrace philosophies that ask them to promote their needs over others. But receiving is a skill that can be learned; it can be developed and strengthened over time.

Learning how to receive will help you feel more nourished and empowered. The ability to receive is, in fact, essential to physical health, psychological balance, and spiritual alignment. Also, being available to receive is part of loving yourself.

You can start small. Opening up yourself to receive is a balance, and one you can master by starting slow. If someone offers to open the door, take it; if you get a "thank you" or receive a compliment, acknowledge it, accept it without deflecting or returning the compliment. These small, simple acts of kindness can help you open up to receive.

It's important to get into the habit of receiving because the universe is trying to deliver your goals to you. Most of us block ourselves from receiving what we really want without even realizing it. I was blocking my self-love from happening by focusing on how it wasn't here yet. It wasn't until I let go of my expectations and allowed myself to open up to receive what the universe had in store for me. 219

After seeing the positive impacts such a small practice had on my life, I was motivated to take it even deeper. So I tried something radical, just to see how it felt. I started to thank myself for just being me.

I would say things like, "Thank you for doing the best you can." "Thank you for trying each day to do your best." Even when I was disappointed with myself, even when I thought I had fallen short, I took myself to a place where I could still be grateful to myself and appreciative of the fact that I had shown up. I had made an effort.

The results of my self-love gratitude practice were surreal. I found inner peace, discovered my life purpose, and developed a genuine love and appreciation for me and life. This is the true power of self-acceptance and love.

It's easy to get confused about this. It's easy to let self-imposed expectations and guilt trick us into believing self-love is selfish. It isn't. It is our innermost need. When we accept ourselves fully and feel gratitude and appreciation for ourselves, we can give to others our time, our energy, and our love more richly. This is the true art and beauty of receiving. You allow yourself to give yourself what you need most. Love and attention.

AS I AM,
instead of how
I think I need to Be.
I AM ENOUGH.

#MeMattersMantra

Show Up as You Are

MY SELF-LOVE EXPERIMENT WAS not an overnight fix but an "experiment." Some days it was a lot easier to stick to the plan. Then, because I am human, I found myself overeating or falling into negative thought patterns. The way to break through to self-love is by focusing on self-compassion and love. Self-loathing and guilt will not serve you in reaching your goal. So you spent a little more than you planned, maybe you ate more than you wanted, or you didn't have enough time to do your creative project. Beating yourself up for failed expectations is not helping you at all. We have to drop the pity party, and we do this by committing to ourselves. You have to commit to yourself. This doesn't mean that you are on point every second of every day; you will stray from your path, you will have setbacks, but when you commit to yourself you are walking alongside yourself as a friend. You are standing by you. You are using faith to pull you forward as you stand side by side with your own self. You are your best friend, and this energy will connect you to your ideal life. What does this mean? This means even when you are breaking down, crying, sad, or feeling lonely and consumed with worry and self-hate, you stand by you. You do not abandon yourself. Abandoning yourself means giving up. Throwing in the towel, saying it's too hard, and sacrificing your true desires by settling for a way of life that doesn't lift you up or serve you. Instead of settling for a life that doesn't feel good, stand by you; become your own pal.

This looks like holding your true self up into the light, with your scars, setbacks, pain, insecurity, and tears all in plain view and hugging yourself, energetically of course. Do not abandon yourself, because in these times of setback you need you more than ever. Stand tall and stand by you. Can you rise up and stand by you? All you need to do is commit to yourself. Choose self-love in every moment. Self-love is not an "oh, when it feels good I will do it" concept, and then when you feel bad you abandon your self-love practice. When you are down and out is when the self-love practice is most important.

> Show up for yourself even in your
> darkest hour. The light you emit—your
> own light—will be your beacon in the
> night guiding the way forward.

Several weeks into my Self-Love Experiment, I experienced the true power of this concept. I realized I had gone a while without feeling self-loathing, guilt, or self-hate. I was able to look in mirrors and feel proud of who I was. I had a moment of celebration; I felt unbounded excitement because I was living a life full of self-love and compassion. This is what I had worked for so many years to achieve. Here I was living it. Then, within twenty-four hours, everything turned upside down. My mood changed as fast as a tropical storm. It took over my emotions, and I felt incredibly depressed, super fat, mad at everything, and incredibly lonely. I was blaming myself for everything and crying randomly throughout the day. Nothing had changed in my life, except I had dropped my guard. I was riding high on the feeling that I was out of the woods and self-love was my new way of life, I had achieved it, then that gave my ego an invitation to swoop in and put my good-feeling self in its place.

After about two days of self-loathing, overeating, and fear, I found myself crying on the bedroom floor. Ashamed at how far off track I felt, how my Self-Love Experiment wasn't working, how I was destined to live a life full of fear and in a fat body, I then heard my inner voice chime in and say, "My dear, stand by you!" I wiped my tears and committed to myself. I said, "Shannon, I am going to stand by you. That means in this moment of weakness, fear stricken and full of self-hate and blame, I stand by you. I will not leave you in this desperation. I am your friend; I am right by your side. You are never alone, dear one. I am going to stand by you."

That moment changed everything for me. Once I committed to myself, my fear and ego voices diminished. They no longer had a playground to play in. My love for self overcame fear, because I invited it in. We have to invite self-love in; we have to open the door of our emotions and say, "Please come in and make yourself comfortable, you are welcome here." Self-love is waiting quietly outside of fear, but like a good friend, it doesn't come over uninvited. Invite self-love in, and do this daily.

Loving yourself is not about flying high on self-love feelings one hundred percent of the time. Loving yourself is not about living a fulfilled and happy life free of worry and setbacks. Loving yourself is indeed the opposite. Living a life full of self-love is committing to yourself and standing by you, even in the setbacks, even in the fear, and when insecurity swoops in and tries to take over, self-love will break through and shine softly as you make it through the

223

pain. You are not alone because you are standing by you. That is the power of the Self-Love Experiment. You allow yourself to fall, and when you do, instead of turning to guilt, blame, or fear, you simply meet yourself where you are. Instead of where you think you should be. You say, "Okay, self-love, let's do this again." So stop beating yourself up and opt for a more compassionate way of being: stand by you.

I STAND BY ME.

#MeMattersMantra

Let me fall if I must.

The one I will become

will catch me.

—BAAL SHEM TOV

PART 6

THE
SELF-LOVE
PRINCIPLES

THROUGHOUT MY SELF-LOVE EXPERIMENT, I started to align with guiding sutras, or principles, if you will. These mini-mantras acted as daily principles to help me align with self-love and joy. This section serves not only as a recap of my experience but also as guiding principles to lead you forward. The entire process of learning how to accept yourself comes back to these guiding truths. Let them guide you in your own Self-Love Experiment.

THE SELF-LOVE PRINCIPLES

1. Accept where you are. It's just a point on your journey and everything about it offers the possibility for further growth.
2. Be who you needed to be when you were younger.
3. Thinking you don't have a choice is a choice.
4. To get what you want, you have to let go of what you don't want.
5. Strive every day to be a better version of you.
6. How you feel is more important than how you look.
7. Things don't happen to you, they happen for you.
8. When you nurture the inside, the outside will flourish.

9. The more *you* you show, the more your life will flow.
10. You get what you focus on.
11. Your dreams are the invisible architecture of your life. Trust them. Honor them.
12. Your relationship with yourself sets the tone for everything in your life.
13. When you heal yourself, you help to heal the world.
14. You are a gift. Remind yourself how lucky you are to be alive.
15. Self-love is not about how you look or what you do; it's about how you live.

Let's dive a little deeper into each one, as it can help you align with your truth.

Accept where you are.

It's just a point on your journey and everything about it offers the possibility for further growth.

* Principle 1 *

YOU CAN RECALL THAT acceptance is the first act of kindness to yourself. We must accept where we are in order to get to where we want to be. For me, I was at war with myself for decades. It wasn't until I accepted myself as I was—my overweight body, my flaws and insecurities, and all my worries and fears—instead of running away in disgust or trying to hide them from others, that I was able to love myself. I needed to change my perspective on myself. Instead of looking at myself as flawed or broken, I started to see each situation, each pain point and insecurity, as a by-product of my growth or a simple situation that was in my life to help me grow. Everything is in our life to help us grow—everything. People, situations, and even insecurities and self-sabotaging habits. What we can learn through our own Self-Love Experiment is that it is all connected. Everything, all the pain, and the heartbreak, and worries that maybe you would never find what you needed or were looking for, it was all in your life for a reason. Each step, one by one, and each book you read, each thing you tried, each relationship you jumped into that didn't work, were all part of the plan as we learn the way on the way. We don't have to see the whole picture; we just have to take one step at a time.

The other day I was talking with two girlfriends. One of them asked me how long it had been since I was in a relationship. I responded almost four years. She looked at me in total shock. I told her I emotionally shut down after my last relationship, I gave up on life and myself, but I smiled and told her I felt ready. After years of self-hate and blame, I dove deep into my Self-Love Experiment and found something I never had before: self-love and acceptance. She asked me, "How do you know you are ready for love now?" I said, "Because I love myself."

This was a relatively new take on life, but it is a reflection of all the work I have done. I showed up for the assignments that were placed in front of me. The moments of extreme self-hate and self-sabotage were all in my life to help me see the purpose in the pain. I started to analyze my life in a way that felt more joyful and uplifting. I was either celebrating a newfound realization, one of growth, or I was in a time of deep growth. For many years, I emotionally beat myself up, and that was a time of deep emotional, spiritual, and even physical growth for me. I started to repeat the mantra: there is purpose to my pain.

233

> ## All pain has a purpose; it is there to guide us to new ways of living and being in the world.

We must believe in the power of growth and the possibilities of tomorrow. If you put in the work and you show up for yourself constantly, what is meant to be yours will find you.

If you can first accept where you are, all of you, the odd, quirky, gloriously beautiful self, you will see the world is a much better place since you showed up for you. Things that once seemed overwhelming, unbearable, and even intimidating suddenly look softer and more peaceful. Simply because you are softer and more peaceful.

Instead of thinking you need to reach a certain feeling, place, or goal, simply ask yourself, "Am I going through something that will help me grow? Or am I celebrating recent growth?" There are always only two states. Allow yourself to be where you are and accept all of your glorious wonder.

Be who you needed to be when you were younger.

* Principle 2 *

THERE IS A PIECE of us that is still young, wounded, and in desperate need of attention and care. Through our Self-Love Experiments we can discover the power of forgiveness. I talked about this in the last section, but it is important to go deeper and mention it again. We all have situations that happen in our lives, and if you were to be honest with yourself you could probably pinpoint the moment in your life when you felt a shift. The shift is the moment you changed perspective. At one point in your life, often as a young child, you felt safe, loved, and secure. Then something happened; your parents started yelling at you, someone may have done something to violate your trust, you saw someone's true colors, and all of a sudden that safe, secure, and loving life felt uncertain and fearful. We adapt by building up emotional walls and overcompensating. We learn new behaviors, such as overeating, overworking, trying to people please, or shying away from conflict in order to make sure we don't find ourselves in these situations again. The good news is that we can redirect our attention to a more loving way of living. You can do this by identifying the situation that caused you so much pain and rewriting the story to a more loving and peaceful outcome. We do this by showing up for our younger self.

I learned the power of showing up for yourself while watching the documentary on Tony Robbins called *I Am Not Your Guru*. In the film Tony Robbins asked participants, "Whose love did you crave most growing up?" I encourage you to ask yourself this key question, as it can lead to a breakthrough. I never asked myself that before. I felt very loved as a child, but when Tony Robbins asked that question, I immediately thought of my dad. When I was younger, I always tried to get my dad to approve of me and love me.

He told me he loved me, but he never really showed it in a way I could understand. He worked a lot, and when he got home from work he was usually really tired. My love tank was full with my mom, but I felt as if a wall was always up between my dad and me. It was difficult for him to express emotions, and as a result, I didn't feel the loving connection I needed. Then I did what most of us do in this situation: I emotionally overcompensated. Tony Robbins then asked, "Who did you have to be for your father?" For me I had to be successful, I dove into my studies and became an overachiever. Because when my father said "I am proud of you," I felt love. It seemed he told me he loved me or that he was proud of me only when I received a good grade or won an award. My father loved sweet treats and potato chips. As a way of bonding with him, I would overstuff myself and eat past capacity as well. I gained a lot of weight as a child. Eating became a way to connect with my father.

At age nine I became extremely overweight, and my father started making comments about my weight. He called me thunder thighs, and although he didn't mean to offend me, that stunned me. That was my moment, my shift, and the time in my life when I emotionally shut down and built up the emotional wall around my heart. I felt ugly, unloved, and extremely unattractive.

My father meant no harm, but I interpreted his words as indicating that I was unlovable. So it is natural that I grew up believing I was ugly, fat, and unlovable. But the little girl, the one who felt unloved by her dad because he couldn't show her love in a way that she needed, never left me. For decades I dated men who could never give me what I wanted. They loved me, I loved them, but I never felt loved, I never felt like they could love me in a way that I really hoped for. I didn't know until my Self-Love Experiment that this is all because of my relationship with my father. The good news is that the fix for this all-too-common situation is simple. First, become aware of the situation that has caused you harm. What happened in your life that

236

shook you to your core? You didn't get what you needed and learned how to adjust your behavior to ensure that never happened again.

> We all have imbalances we need to heal. The way to do it is to reclaim vulnerability and feel your feelings.

Once we address the root cause and give the little us permission to feel and express our truth, the adult version of us can heal. I found self-love. I don't blame my father at all; in fact, if you were to have asked me prior to my Self-Love Experiment if I had family issues I would have said no way. That is the thing about these childhood wounds; sometimes they don't manifest into real grudges, and most of the time we aren't even aware of their impact. However, we feel these wounds energetically. The Self-Love Experiment gave me the real gift of identifying the root cause of my suffering. It all comes back to a lack of love that is usually initiated by a parent or other family member. When using Tony Robbins's method to heal family patterns, ask yourself these key questions:

1. Whose love did you crave most growing up?
2. Who did you have to be for that person?
3. What do you blame this person for?
4. What gift did this person give you? (Without the situation you wouldn't be who you are.)
5. Forgive them and release the pain from the past.
6. Celebrate who you are.

You see, our biggest problem is that we think our problems are a big deal. We feel as though we shouldn't have them.

All problems help us grow.

It is all connected, and the pain we feel as children is part of our souls' growth and ultimate life lessons. We all have different lessons. But self-love is always the result of overcoming these painful situations from childhood.

My father gave me a great gift. Through his lack of attention, I learned how to love myself. If he was the father I needed him to be, I wouldn't be the woman I am today. I had to experience a father who didn't express emotion openly so that I could learn how to love myself and not need others to validate my own existence. I am thankful for him.

Who can you thank? Who hurt you so much that you had to change and learn how to adopt new ways of being? Instead of blaming this person for all the pain, why not thank them for all the good as well?

I tried this, and instead of saying I blame my dad for making me feel fat and unlovable when I eat food, for not telling me I am beautiful or enough as I am, for not being there when I needed him most, I switched it to thanking him for the good things, too. I thank my dad for being the one man I could love despite his lack of attention and ability to express his feelings. I thank my dad for giving me the tools to learn how to love myself. I thank my dad for caring so much about me that he emotionally supports me in all my dreams and endeavors. Thank your past. Instead of blaming others for hurting you, can you thank them for the good they have caused in your life? Because all problems are pathways and every person you meet is in your life to help you grow. The person's love you craved the most growing up is the root cause of the self-love you seek. Revisit your past, and give yourself the love you never got as an adult.

So the final question is: Who do you need to be for younger you?

Thinking you don't have a choice is a choice.

* Principle 3 *

I LEARNED A VALUABLE lesson during my Self-Love Experiment, which is that we always have a choice. And when you feel as though you don't have a choice, that is indeed a choice. For years I felt as though I couldn't lose weight, I was doomed to be fat, and I was unlovable. I argued that I didn't have a choice, no matter what I did; I was stuck in my frustration. This was a choice, and that choice served me for many years. What I mean is, being overweight actually helped me for a little while. I was broken down after my relationship ended, and I was starting to become more public with my writing and speaking career. The extra weight served as padding for me for a few years. I understand its purpose now. But while I was in it, when I was overweight and hating my body, I felt as though I didn't have a choice. But this kept me stuck. It kept me playing the victim card and feeling insecure. This didn't serve me. But eventually I started to see everything in my life as a choice and started to make deliberate choices. If you make eating ice cream for breakfast a choice, instead of falling victim to your "lack" of self-control, then you will became empowered. And as you feel more empowered you start to take more steps to become healthier, which will lead you to self-love.

We always have a choice. Thinking we don't keeps us stuck.

Ask yourself if you feel as though you don't have a choice. Usually there is an area of our life that we feel stuck and blocked in.

240

We can't seem to get ahead or make progress. What I learned was: this was indeed progress. I will say it again: even when we feel stuck, we are actually in a time of transformational growth. The goal is to look at your life as ever expanding, constantly presenting you with opportunities to become more of who you really are. When you feel as though you don't have a choice, you are stuck, and you may feel trapped by life circumstances. This pattern does not help you see results. Instead of hiding out in this fear and feeling as though you can't make a change, start to ask yourself, "What change can I make?" Ask yourself a more empowering question and you will see the results you seek. For every situation you are experiencing, there are choices you made that led to the current circumstances. Look at your choices as opportunities. There are no wrong choices, because every choice you make helps you learn more about who you are and what you want and need in life. If you don't like your current situation, you can make new choices and get new results.

To get what you want, you have to let go of what you don't want.

* Principle 4 *

HOW MUCH STRESS ARE you carrying around? Do you feel burdened by life's circumstances and emotional issues? Becoming more grounded and happy starts with letting go of worry and stress. I learned this in my own journey, through overcoming drug addictions, healing myself from depression, and walking away from a career in corporate America to follow my heart and be a successful writer and life coach. In order to become the person I am today, I had to let go of a lot of things.

Physically, spiritually, and emotionally, I had to learn how to let go of the person I thought I should be in order to be the person I really wanted to be. Letting go of anything in life can be a little scary, but it can also be an amazing act of self-love.

Letting go of my worries and stress made a difference for me; of course I still dip in and out of some of my stress jar from time to time, but I've found this list to be a good reminder of what I need to strive for each day in order to reach unlimited happiness.

In my last book, *Adventures for Your Soul*, I shared the powerful process of learning how to let go. I call it the Sweet Surrender approach. We often worry that we have somehow gotten off course. We think that perhaps our life is off track, and we have made mistakes that are unfixable. Maybe you worry that you aren't quite where you think you should be, whether it is the job you thought you'd have by this age, the relationship status, or where you would be living at this time in your life. If you aren't where you thought you'd be, you may feel like a failure. I call this a destination disaster, the feeling that our life is off track. This never-ending cycle keeps us constantly reaching for expectations that we have placed upon ourselves. These expectations are usually derived from unmet needs, and our mind tells us this is what we must do, be, accomplish, in order to be fulfilled. If, for any reason, life doesn't go along with our plans, we take the blame and feel like a failure.

Through the Self-Love Experiment we learn the true power of letting go. When you let go of who you *think* you are supposed to be, the universe can swoop in and help you become who you are really *meant* to be. If you feel as though you are off track and constantly playing catch-up to some ideal set forth for your life, the best thing to do is Sweet Surrender.

Surrender is not giving up or saying that everything is perfectly okay; it is the willingness to let yourself energetically off the hook of trying to control the outcome. It is exhausting to try to be in charge all the time, which is why Sweet Surrender is your key to happiness. Surrendering is recognizing and accepting what you can't change. We do this by releasing expectations.

We try to control our lives because of what we think is going to happen if we don't; basically, our control is sourced from fear. Control is the result of being attached to a specific outcome—one we are certain is the best for us. I often say when we try to control a situation we are trying to play God. When we are attached to an outcome, the universe cannot come in and help give us what we really need. The truth: the energy behind surrender accomplishes so much more than the desperate energy of control. Think about the difference between the two. Control energy is tight, restricted, and often manic. Your mind may shift from the past to the future very quickly as you try to figure out the solution. Now switch to surrender mode; you are calm, peaceful, and connected to your truest self.

You are more present in the moment, and you can see there are things happening behind the scenes to help support your desires and needs. You trust. You let go of the attachment by being present in this moment. If you are obsessing and micromanaging all the details of your life; this is a guarantee that you are in your own way. Step into the Sweet Surrender by going inward and repeating this mantra:

> *I allow my life to unfold naturally.*
> *I trust all is in the right order.*
> *The universe supports my desires and me.*

Ask yourself, "What am I holding on to?" What are you afraid to release but know in letting go you will have what you want? It could be a person, situation, or thought pattern. For me it was all of the above.

In your Self-Love Experiment, be willing to let go of the person you were, in order to become who you are really meant to be. I was willing to let go of the belief that I am unlovable and not good enough, and self-love rushed in. Self-love is possible, but we must let go of what we don't want in order to get what we do want.

The only question that remains is: What are you willing to let go of?

Strive
every day to
be a better
version of you.

* Principle 5 *

YOU'VE PROBABLY BEEN ABLE to see a theme in this book and the Self-Love Experiment, and that is to just keep showing up and doing the best you can. This doesn't mean you push, sweat, and pull your way to the top and step all over others to get ahead; it's the opposite. I actually mean you show up for you, as you are in each moment. This means you look setbacks, insecurities, fears, and doubts in the eye and say, "I see you, I am here, I show up despite you." You keep going and honor the process of becoming your best self. Each day is an opportunity to be more of who you really are, but you can do this only when you are kind to yourself along the way.

I used to stress out over my daily routine. I would wake up with anxiety and feel crushing guilt from all the mishaps and mistakes from the day before. I never felt like I was where I was supposed to be, so I was always trying to catch up to some illusion of what I thought would make me happy. This all changed when I let go of pretenses and expectations around how my life is supposed to look and instead just reframed my focus. I started to say, "As long as I am doing the best I can, that is enough." And guess what? Some days, "the best I can" was just making it through the day. There were times during my Self-Love Experiment when I stayed on the couch and watched Netflix, I overate and didn't drink enough water, nor did I get enough exercise, and in those moments of what would have been despair, I simply said, "For today, I am trying, I simply did the best I could." This is called balance. This is not giving up on yourself or settling; this is called self-compassion. And I knew that in order to become my own best friend I needed to be gentle with myself even on the days when I felt like a giant failure.

Because something magically happens when you let go of pretenses and expectations around being perfect. You stop trying so hard to please everyone and instead focus your attention on pleasing yourself. Once we let go of thinking our life has to be perfect and we have to look a certain way or be a certain way, we can find peace. The only question to ask yourself is, "How can I show up for myself more today?"

How You feel
is more
important
than how you
look.

* Principle 6 *

A GUIDING PRINCIPLE FOR our Self-Love Experiment is to stop focusing so much on our looks and how others perceive us. Before my experiment, I spent so much time trying to fit in and be accepted, but I didn't accept myself. So all my efforts were wasted. When I started my Self-Love Experiment, yes, I was overweight, and I felt ugly and frumpy, but I realized the main problem was my focusing on that as a problem. I promised to take my attention off of what wasn't working and focus on how I wanted to feel. I turned inward and asked, "How do I want to feel?" Even though I was overweight, I said to myself, "I want to feel comfortable in my skin. I want to feel vibrant and healthy."

I started to focus fully on these key core feelings, and soon my outward world changed. Because I was focusing fully on how I wanted to feel instead of on how I looked, my habits began to change as well. I joined a new gym, one that had a more holistic approach to wellness, and I started shopping at organic food stores and cooking more at home. I made small shifts such as taking the stairs instead of elevators, or I would park my car far from the entrance so I could walk more. Soon enough, my body and mental space improved dramatically. I lost more physical weight and I felt vibrant. The key for me was to find activities I enjoyed—things that didn't feel like a chore but brought me joy. I love spinning, so when I traveled I made it a point to do workouts in different cities. I went to cycling studios in New York, Berlin, California, etc. These small shifts made showing up for myself a lifestyle, not just a one-hit-wonder approach to solving a problem. Once I let go of looking at my overweight body as a problem, I was able to reach my desired feelings of self-love faster.

The only thing holding us back is our own thoughts about our capabilities. I thought because I was overweight I couldn't do things, like run or go on dates or fall in love or be seen as attractive or lovable. I was focusing on my body size and how big it was, but by switching my focus to what I could do and how I wanted to feel, things felt better.

Once we let go of our limitations, we are able to do, be, and have more.

In putting my attention on feeling good, things radically changed for me. One day it came together for me, and suddenly it all became so clear. It was like a bolt of lightning came down and zapped me into clarity. I call it the aha moment. I had an aha moment when I realized I was obsessing about my Instagram following. Normally, I don't give much thought about my numbers on social media; I've built a beautiful community of loving and dedicated people who are all committed to living with more joy and love. The numbers grow at a natural pace, which is nice, because I do want to grow the community. But this particular three-day stretch, I was obsessing. I was on Instagram all the time, trying to focus on how to grow my fan page and get more likes. This habit started to distract me from living my life. When I was with friends and out in public, instead of enjoying their company, I was on Instagram, trying to reach more people to increase my likes. I woke up first thing in the morning and looked at my account to see if the engagement was up . . . this is the hidden side of social media. It can consume you if you don't catch yourself. Well, I remember I was sitting on my balcony one day when it clicked: I was obsessing over my social media because I had found body love. I was no longer obsessing about my body or my physical weight. I loved myself and was starting to feel really happy in my life. I felt more peace, so naturally the mind was going to try to find something else to worry about. Because I was no longer focusing or obsessing about my own insecurities, my ego swooped in and found something new to obsess about: my Instagram following.

My newfound obsession was just an old habit of worry. I always needed something to worry about, and because I had self-love, even though I was no longer thinking about my body size or how I looked physically, I had just replaced one habit for another. Social media is still about "how you look," and I had tricked myself into thinking that if I had more followers, I would be better known or more liked. I was striving for some internal competition that didn't make much sense. In my moment of clarity, I let go of the thought that I needed more followers to be happy, and I washed my hands of trying to grow my social media and obsessing over "how things looked" and focused on how I wanted to feel. When I was honest, obsessing about my Instagram wasn't about the number of followers—it was about what I thought that represented. If I had more followers, then maybe people would recognize me as a serious, influential author, maybe I would have more industry recognition. But none of that is important because even when I got recognition, if I didn't love myself, I still felt as though it wasn't enough. The real question is, How do you want to feel? What is the feeling you are looking for that you seek? When I asked this, it was clear I wanted to feel proud. I wanted to know my work was making a difference in the lives of others. I stopped putting my attention on the numbers on my social media and focused on feeling proud of myself. As I became my own biggest cheerleader, the outside world started to reflect this. I received more e-mails and comments from people expressing their heartfelt appreciation for my articles and books. My social media numbers started to grow, not just a little—

by a ton. Within five months, I grew my Facebook community @ShannonKaiserWrites by more than sixty thousand people. I believe wholeheartedly that this is because I was aligned and focusing on the feeling of being proud of myself and reaching self-love. I was aligned with my true self. When I loved myself, others could feel this, and this energy is attractive. Even if it is through a computer screen, people know genuine when they see it. It is an essence. So focus on the feeling, not on how you look, and you will see radical results as well. The question for you is: How do you want to feel?

Principle 7:

Things don't happen to you, they happen for you.

* Principle 7 *

IMAGINE, IF YOU WILL, that everything in your life is orchestrated by design for you. Every person you meet is a character in your life adventure, every situation is in your life to help with the plot and create a little drama and a good twist. Perhaps the most riveting principle is to understand that situations, problems, and things don't happen to you, but they do indeed happen for you. The beauty of this concept is that everything you are going through, everything you have gone through, and everything you will go through is part of a bigger plan. It is essentially all for you. Everything in our life is by design, to give us lessons and opportunities to apply our knowledge to new situations. Neale Donald Walsch says it wonderfully:

> It is okay to be at a place of struggle. Struggle is just another word for growth. Even the most evolved beings find themselves in a place of struggle now and then. In fact, struggle is a sure sign to them they are expanding; it is their indication of real and important progress. The only one who doesn't struggle is the one who doesn't grow. So if you are struggling right now, see it as a terrific sign—celebrate your struggle.[19]

When we struggle we can look at it as if things are happening to us or for us. Remember everything, *all* of it, happens for you. This idea is based on a spiritual principle to help us see the growth opportunities in each phase of our life. I spent decades thinking that I was unlucky, and stayed miserable. I'd think things like, "How can my friends eat whatever they want and be so thin, while I have to watch my diet so much? I am doomed to be fat." During our Self-

Love Experiment, we can discover the power of owning our life situations and taking responsibility for what we see. If you don't like the outcome you are living, you have a choice. The same way you made choices that led you into the situation that you aren't thrilled about, you can make choices to get out. This is a freeing thought, as it gives you the power to own your life and take full responsibility for your own creative adventure. I've definitely talked about this principle throughout the book, but think about your own life and how you can look at situations as opportunities that happen to you, instead of setbacks. What if you adopted the mind-set that everything is for your greatest good, all of it is happening for you? This certainly will help you feel more grace and ease through difficult times. It will also help you see troubling situations as opportunities to learn more about yourself, and you will soon see how they fit into your greater life plan. Ask yourself, "What good is coming out of the current situations that are troubling me?"

Principle 8:

When you nurture the inside, the outside will flourish.

* Principle 8 *

THIS PRINCIPLE, ONE OF my favorites, is that when you nurture the inside, the outside will not only function, it *will flourish*. This was clear when I turned my attention inward and focused on caring for me. Make your self-care a priority, and your outside world will start to reflect this. Think about your own life and what you are putting emphasis on. Do you say you want to be healthy but continue to fall into self-sabotaging habits of overeating or avoiding moving your body? Maybe you want to find a relationship but focus so much on being seen and being in the right place at the right time that maybe you aren't paying much attention to your inner world. What I mean by "inner world" is your relationship with self. I took a four-year sabbatical from dating and wasn't open to romantic love because I wanted to make sure my inner world was nurtured and cared for. I wanted to really feel self-love and respect for me. Only then could I attract the type of partner who loves himself, too. There's no time limitation on healing. It may take you four decades, four months, or four days. The time isn't important, as it is different for everyone; the only thing that matters is that you stay consistent in your choice to heal. The more I focused on caring for myself with love and compassion, the quality of men I met improved. I started to meet men who were spiritual and healthy and cared about humanity. Men who were less judgmental and committed to making their dreams come true. Men who were open-minded and dedicated to personal growth and living a life they were proud of. These types of men were imaginary before my experiment; I didn't think they existed, but after I found self-love, I discovered that we attract what we put out into the world. So when I truly and really wholeheartedly loved myself, I could then meet more people who did as well. I say "found" self-love because it really was lost. It is something we all have, but we lose our way, we stray from it, and that keeps us blocked. But even with that said, self-love isn't something you find, because it is actually a part of us always. It is within us; we just have to peel back the layers to let it shine through.

For your own life, ask yourself these powerful questions to help you reach self-love:

What are the qualities of my relationships between others
    and myself?
How can I nurture myself more?
What do I need that I am not currently getting?
How can I give myself what I need most?

The more YOU, you show, the more your life will flow.

* Principle 9 *

I WAS MADE FUN of a lot as a kid, and other kids always called me weird when I was growing up. I used to get so frustrated when people called me weird. So as an adult it drove me nuts when people said I was weird. All through my twenties, if men I dated or friends ever called me weird, it would trigger my childhood insecurity and I got so offended. Here's the thing about being offended:

We get offended only because something in the comment or situation reflects a place that still needs to be healed.

Otherwise, we wouldn't be bothered. We would not be affected at all because it wouldn't trigger anything. So if you get offended often or have a situation or person who really hurts your feelings, it is because there is still a piece of you that has not accepted the situation or come to terms with it. When people called me weird, I felt insecure and hated it. I'd get mad and shut down emotionally. "Weird" to me meant an outcast, someone who is off and doesn't fit in. My biggest desire was to fit in, because I never got that as a child. But self-love gives you the gift of acceptance. The other day a person called me weird, and for the first time in my entire life I didn't feel offended or have the need to defend myself. I smiled and said, "Yep, this is me." Because I realized what I was doing wasn't odd at all—that was just this person's perception. When we accept ourselves, we arrive at a place where we no longer need others' approval. I am at a place where I am comfortable with myself and my life, so her comment had no effect on me. Your old triggers and insecurities fall away. That is the true power of self-love. You accept who you are and love yourself for who you are. If other people think I am weird, that doesn't really concern me. I love me, and that is all that matters. This is because I learned the power of showing more of the real me. Only then could my life really flow.

The trick is to focus on loving and caring for yourself. Love your insecurities and show more of you. The more you show of your real self, the easier it will be to align with people who want to be around you and like you. In an earlier section, I told you about my phase when I went through an obsession with social media and trying to grow my following. One of the reasons I was able to stop obsessing and reach more people naturally was because I made the decision to show more of me. I stopped trying to post and say things I thought people wanted me to say and I started to say what I really wanted and felt. This helped people connect with me more. As I started to do this experiment of expressing and showing the real me, I noticed the natural ability I had to connect with others. All of a sudden, things didn't feel forced. More opportunities came to me, and I felt more connected to my true self. The more authentic I was with my messages, the easier it was for people to find and connect with me. Like attracts like, so naturally before my Self-Love Experiment, when I didn't fully accept myself, it was hard to feel connected to my readers and audience. But as I wrote this book and shared my process more openly, I found true love. In sharing this journey with others, I felt more connected to my own life and my readers and coaching clients, and they in turn shared that they could relate to me more easily. It's because I was finally being real and honest with myself and putting the real me out there into the world. Instead of hiding away behind my fear and insecurities, I shined. People often comment

262

on my energy and how joyful I am to be around. I met a woman once in an entrepreneur-training program who said she was very nervous around me when she first met me. She thought my approach to life about focusing on the good and choosing happiness was an act and too good to be true. She even said, "Your enthusiasm for life was so hard to handle. But as I get to know you, I feel it, I see it, and I know it is genuine. And I want to be around you more because you make me feel good about myself."

This is the power of real, honest, raw self-love. When you love yourself and feel good about who you are, this reflects outward and gives others permission to be happy with themselves as well.

The only thing left for you to do is to focus on being more you. Stop hiding out in the shadows of your potential and shed the layers of fear to reveal your glorious, awesome, beautiful self. The more *you* that you show, the more your life will flow. Ask yourself, "In what area of my life can I reveal more of who I really am?"

You get what you focus on.

* Principle 10 *

IT'S IMPORTANT TO RECAP the theme of our Self-Love Experiment and this entire book. The overarching connector between every section in this book and my experience is that our thoughts are important and what you focus on matters. This principle is a gentle reminder that your focus determines your results. People often ask me how I am able to manifest things so quickly. I manifest goals rapidly because I focus my full attention on what I want. I do not waste time with thoughts that don't bring me joy. Think about where you are focusing your attention and align with what you want.

An example of this is my own experiences with dating. It had been more than four years since I had gone out on a date, and many of my single friends were all on Tinder and other dating websites. They went on dates often and told me all about the fun they had. And they all reminded me that this was how people met partners nowadays—it was all online. I had so much resistance to using a dating app or online dating service to help me find love because I want things to be natural. I may be old-fashioned, but I still believe you can meet people while out doing what you love. I admit I was stubborn, but the thought of joining online dating in any form brought up so many fears of people judging me and having me judge others. It got to the point where my friends were begging me to try online dating because they knew how much I wanted love. During my Self-Love Experiment, I opened myself back up to the possibility of falling in love. Again my friends told me *I had to get online* in order to find someone, but I refused to believe them or listen to them. I knew if I focused on what I wanted, I would eventually get what I wanted, which in this case was a potential partner or meeting someone nice while doing what I loved. I like to experience life and play with the world, and I was confident I would meet people without having to go online to date. I also held the belief that what is meant for you will always find a way. One night I was out with my girlfriends, eating dinner outside on the sidewalk patio of a restaurant. They were telling me about their Tinder dates of the week. I said, "I just want to meet someone while I am out having fun and doing what I love. I believe it can happen." Then thirty seconds later a man walking by stopped to look at the menu on the wall and asked if he could sit at the corner of our picnic table bench. He told us he lived in the neighborhood and had never eaten there before. We invited him to join us, and we had a good time. We went out together the following night. It didn't go any further than one date, but my point is, I believed I could meet men off-line, and the universe brought me a man. It happens that fast when you believe. The only work for you is to believe fully in the power of your dreams. Remember that what you want, wants you, too. With this belief, you will be unstoppable. Ask yourself, "What am I focused on? What do I want?"

Your dreams are the invisible architecture of your life.

Trust them.

Honor them.

* Principle 11 *

SO MANY OF US have dreams tucked inside our hearts, but fear
and worry stop us from pursuing them. Excuses keep us stuck and
locked into fear, which is the opposite of love. An excuse is just fear
blocking us from potential. We can choose to focus on an excuse
and then it becomes our reality—as in we believe the excuses, such
as "I can't do that because I am too old or not educated enough or
not smart enough"—or we can choose to see it for what it is, a fear-
based thought, and disengage with it so we can let love lead the
way. When you identify your excuses, you can see clearly where
you have been holding yourself back. When we let go of excuses, we
can see the results fast. As far as reaching self-love, many people
think they can't love themselves if they are single. We think we
can't love ourselves if we are overweight or underweight. We can't
truly accept ourselves until we consistently have more money in
the bank. These are excuses. We have to identify them so we can
see them for what they really are: fear. And anytime we have fear,
it is just an invitation for more love. I took my giant excuses, and I
sent them love. It looked something like this:

> **EXCUSE 1:** *I can't love myself if I am overweight.*
>
> > Love thought: Self-love is not about how you look
> > but how you live.

> **EXCUSE 2:** *A man won't love me if I am overweight.*
>
> > Love thought: You are beautiful as you are, and
> > there are many people who want to be with your
> > genuine, authentic, gorgeous self.

EXCUSE 3: *I can't do what I really want until I have more money.*

> Love thought: You don't need a lot of money to be fulfilled and happy.

You get the picture. I invite you to try this method for yourself. Look at your excuses, write them down, then counter them with a loving thought. Because most often it is only your excuses that are standing in the way of you living your dream life. Your fear-based thoughts are blocking you from reaching self-love, but when you approach these excuses with loving thoughts, you will see forward momentum and more positive results.

Remember, our excuses often seem real. They are powerful like that; they will trick you into thinking they are not excuses. All you have to do is ask yourself, "Is this thought limiting me?" For instance, I have a good friend who has been writing for more than a decade. She has four published books and often tells me, "There is no money in writing books; you can't make a living doing it." This is a thought that she believes is real, but it is also an excuse. Because it is limiting her, this belief that doing what you love—in her case, writing books—can't bring you money is fear-based. It's also based on her past. A reality she's lived through. But the reality is that no matter what your current circumstances, if you can picture and imagine your life the way you want it to be, if you can think about it being better, then you can indeed create it. I had that belief when I first left my corporate job, but I quickly identified it as a limiting belief, that you can't make a living doing what you love, and an excuse that was not serving me. So I turned it into love by repeating the mantra "I make a fabulous living doing what I love." And today I am writing the final chapter of this book in Paris, France, because I can travel and work from anywhere in the world, and I do indeed make a fabulous living doing what I love. I found results as soon as

I let go of my excuses, and you will, too. But we have to commit to our dreams, and we do this by focused intentions. So the next and only question to ask yourself is, "What thoughts do I have that are holding me back, and how can I turn them into love?"

Your relationship
with yourself
sets the tone
for everything
in your
life.

Principle 12

AFTER WALKING AWAY FROM a secure corporate job, leaving depression, drug addiction, and eating disorders behind, I was ready to step into my new life. And yet, before my Self-Love Experiment, I found my romantic relationships were still chaotic and loaded with insecurity and pain.

No matter how hard I tried, my love life was still a battlefield. For the majority of my life, I had been dependent on the attention of men. My relationships were transitory, and my self-esteem was based on the person I was with. In past relationships, I was desperate to feel loved and therefore ignored every red flag. I was the girl who sacrificed everything in an effort to please my man.

No matter which man I was involved with, the patterns were always the same: a roller coaster of drama fueled by misunderstandings, anger, and regretful words. Every once in a while, a loving moment would peek through, but those moments were fleeting and always followed by defensive accusations. I wanted love so much that I convinced myself that this was how relationships were supposed to work. But during my Self-Love Experiment, I began to realize that how I treat myself is how others will treat me. I saw the pattern and realized I needed to quit bad relationships for good. What I wanted was a healthy relationship. What I needed was inner peace. What I was looking for was self-love. What I tried was celibacy. My intention for starting a one-year romance detox was to be able to feel beautiful without a man having to prove it to me. My rules: no dating, no kissing, and no sex! The first few months of singlehood were excruciatingly painful. A euphoric high was quickly followed by a sad loneliness. At times the loneliness took over and hindered my ability to function. Even though I was doing the work and showing up for myself, I still held on to resentment. On some level I felt like such a failure because I couldn't even keep a relationship working right. But after one year, it became clear that I wasn't ready to date, so my one year turned into four. Reflecting on my dating sabbatical, I've gained tremendous insight into who I am and what I really need in life.

Before my experiment, I filled my world with inappropriate relationships in an effort to feel loved and worthwhile. I stayed in relationships way past their expiration dates, and I fell in love with men who were really unhealthy for me.

Taking time off from the distraction of looking for love has allowed me to find true, unconditional love, the kind of love that I could only find within myself. Maya Angelou said, "You alone are enough. You have nothing to prove to anybody." When we are in relationships, so many of us work so hard to prove our lovability and worth. We overextend ourselves because we fear losing the love of the person we are with. Through my Self-Love Experiment, I have recognized that I am enough just as I am. I don't have to try to be someone else to get people to like me or to keep someone in love with me. The same can happen for you when you stop allowing others to treat you anything less than you deserve.

Before my Self-Love Experiment, this girl was angry, afraid, insecure, and stuck. Today my life is fueled by compassion, purpose, love, and joy. I am in the best relationship of my life, and I am still single. The way we treat ourselves sets the tone for everything else in our life. As I started to raise my own vibration with loving energy, I attracted quality relationships into my life. I built a solid group of friends, many of them entrepreneurs who also loved to travel and focus on their dreams. Life becomes easier when we treat ourselves more kindly. When you treat yourself with love and respect, other people will treat you the same way. And once you begin, here is an extra-credit question: How can you treat yourself even better?

Principle 13:

When you heal yourself, you help to heal the World.

* Principle 13 *

TAKE A DEEP BREATH IN. Feel it all? That's life, the beautiful life that comes with showing up for yourself and believing in who you are. When you dedicate time to healing yourself, you will grow and feel more aligned with your best self, but you also will help the world. What I learned in my Self-Love Experiment is that when we heal ourselves and focus on caring for our own side of the street, we help the entire world. First, because there is one less person suffering on the planet, but second, we send out more loving, kind energy, and we can all agree that this is what the world needs a little more of.

Have you ever noticed that "healthy self" broken apart says "heal thyself"?

To focus on health is to focus on healing. We all have situations, problems, and thoughts that cause us pain. Focusing on healing ourselves is a key component to self-love. But focus on your healing with compassion and care. Some people get sick or feel off track and beat themselves up emotionally for not being healthy or further along. Many of us feel as though something is wrong with us if we aren't cured. I felt like my lack of self-love and extreme body hate made me less of a person. It seemed everyone else had it all figured out and were put together, but I was off track and behind. Comparing yourself to others is not the way to heal yourself. You have your own unique journey and plan. Your healing is not dependent on anything other than your own willingness to show up and be present for your own life. In meditation the other day, a loud inner voice said to me, "The degree to which you participate in your life is in direct proportion to the amount of healing that can occur." This means instead of focusing on healing and wondering